A Zest
for Life

Alexander Keiller Museum

A Zest for Life

the story of Alexander Keiller

Lynda J. Murray

MORVEN BOOKS

I DEDICATE THIS BOOK TO MY BROTHER STEPHEN

First published in the United Kingdom in 1999 by:
Morven Books,
16 Templars Firs,
Wootton Bassett,
Swindon SN4 7EN

ISBN 0 9536039 0 3

Typeset in 11/13 pt Garamond
Typesetting and design by John Chandler
Printed by Salisbury Printing, Greencroft Street, Salisbury SP1 1JF

CONTENTS

PREFACE

Alasdair Whittle

IN THIS BOOK, Lynda Murray gives us, for the first time, a full and rounded account of the life and work of Alexander Keiller. Many people involved or interested in archaeology will know a little about the man, especially his successive campaigns at Windmill Hill and Avebury in Wiltshire. Having had the good fortune myself to carry out further research excavations at the great Neolithic causewayed enclosure on Windmill Hill, I have had the opportunity to find out more detail about Keiller through notebooks and letters from the 1920s and 1930s, but it has been reading this book which has given me for the first time the whole story of an extraordinary life. To record this biography, Lynda Murray has worked for years on her own, and I should like warmly to salute her achievement. *me too*

Apart from its general interest and readability, this book is important in two ways. First, it gives us a detailed account of the work of a significant figure in the development of British and not just Wiltshire archaeology in the 1920s and 1930s. As Christopher Evans and Niall Sharples have shown recently, there is a lot to learn about this phase, to which Keiller contributed much. As just one example, Joshua Pollard has been able as part of our forthcoming report to reconstruct considerable detail about the 1920s excavations at Windmill Hill, which is a tribute to the scope and ambition of Keiller.

Secondly, this book gives us a sense of the whole man, in his context. Readers will decide for themselves whether they would have loved or hated Keiller, or both, but for a fuller account of archaeology's own history, which still affects how we think and what we do today in the discipline, we require more studies of this kind. In coping with Keiller, in both literal and metaphorical senses, Lynda Murray has helped to meet this need.

School of History and Archaeology,
Cardiff University

Somebody needs to do the Mary Diaries — he deserves it too.

vii

ACKNOWLEDGEMENTS

This work is published with the assistance of the Michael Sedgwick Memorial Trust. Founded in memory of the famous motoring researcher and author Michael Sedgwick (1926-1983), the Trust is a registered charity to encourage new research and the recording of motoring history. Suggestions for future projects, and donations, should be sent to the Honorary Secretary of the Michael Sedgwick Memorial Trust c/o the John Montagu Building, Beaulieu, Hampshire, SO42 7ZN, England.

In addition a publication grant from the Marc Fitch Fund is most gratefully acknowledged.

This book began as an interest which stemmed from the apparent lack of published information regarding the life of Alexander Keiller. I had moved to Wiltshire in 1989, and was delighted to find Avebury almost on my doorstep. A lifelong interest in archaeology drew me naturally to the Museum, and it was there that my quest was born. The erstwhile curator, Stanley Jenkins, made available to me the wealth of Keiller correspondence in the archive. I read through it all, box upon box, and from there set about tracing other sources. The first reply to my early enquiries was from the late Denis Grant King in 1990, and my first interview was in 1991 with the late Stuart Piggott.

It was not until 1994 that I decided my accumulated notes ought to be written up, and although the road has been a long and winding one, it has been an interesting experience. I have not looked back since.

The following people helped me to piece together what we know of Keiller's story: Dennis Grant King ; Professor Thurstan Shaw; Norman Cook; Leslie V Grinsell; Stuart Piggott; Aubrey Burl; Mary Wood ; Ian Keiller; Patricia Keiller, NZ; Ann Keiller-Greig; Michael Ware, NMM, Beaulieu; Veteran Car Club; Mrs Julie M Bate et al, The Bugatti Trust; Michael Brisby; Malcolm Jeal; MG Car Club Ltd.; Citroen Car Club; Traction Owners Club; Winifred Jarman & Mrs Kemble; Mrs Ovens (nee Perry); Eric Brown, Stakis Balmoral; Susan Palmer; Hilary Howard (for suggesting the title); Michael Pitts; The Dundee Courier; Basingstoke Library; Eton College Register; Hazelwood Preparatory School, Limpsfield; SCGB; Fleet Air Arm Museum; Society of Antiquaries, Scotland; Richard Calvocoressi, National Gallery of Scotland, Edinburgh; Naval Records Office; County Records Office, Trowbridge; Ski Club of Great Britain; PRO, Kew, London; PRO, Edinburgh; Leslie Ferguson, RCAHMS; Pamela Colman, Devizes Museum; Chris Chandler, NMR, Swindon (RCHME); English Heritage; The National Trust; David Davidge; Mike Powell; Chris Gingell; and John Chandler .

fancy!

For those who made my road a difficult one to follow, I thank you anyway for giving me more determination to complete this project, and for those whose names I have omitted in error, my apologies.

Many of my sources are acknowledged in the references, but there are also those who deserve a special thank you, each for different reasons. These I list below: My family, for putting up with my writing, bad temper and distraction, and constant trips away for research purposes; Stanley Jenkins, previous curator of the Alexander Keiller Museum, and my original key to the Archive there; Moira Gittos of the Fleet Air Arm Museum for answering my queries on Keiller's military career with unerring enthusiasm; Alasdair Whittle, for his encouragement when I had all but decided to give up; Gilfrid Day of the SCGB for help above and beyond the call of duty; Bill Mathew, for keeping me on the right track with the family history when I was being swayed by myths; Julian Cope, for his most excellent itinerary of *o dear!* recumbent stone circles which gave me a wonderful introduction to them; Anthony Darrall, for his patience and technical support in the face of all adversity; Sharon Darrall for Scotland, and for being an excellent interviewer when words failed me.

And finally, to Ros Cleal and Clare Conybeare of the Alexander Keiller Museum, for being supportive throughout, and for being justly critical editors, but to Ros especially - I am deeply indebted for her patience with my questions and queries, and, in the closing stages of my work, her invaluable assistance and advice. Thanks Ros.

PICTURE ACKNOWLEDGEMENTS

Fig 2 by kind permission, Dundee County Council Central Library.

Figs.3, 4,20,21,56 attributed to Sharon Darrall, with thanks, and the author.

Fig. 5 attributed to the Dundee Advertiser, courtesy of D C Thomson & Co Ltd

Figs. 6,7,13,16,32,55 appear by kind permission of the Wiltshire Archaeological and Natural History Society Library, and with the assistance of the Alexander Keiller Museum.

Figs. 8, 14, by kind permission of the National Motor Museum, Beaulieu, with the assistance of the Michael Sedgwick Memorial Trust.

Fig 11, by kind permission of 'The Scotsman'

Figs. 12,15,17,18,19,22-24,26,27,33-51,Back cover, and frontispiece, by kind permission of Alexander Keiller Museum

Fig 48 appears by kind permission of Margaret Nurse

Front Cover photo by kind permission of Ski Club of Great Britain.

1
INTRODUCTION

IT IS A SIMPLE ENOUGH task to determine where begins the life of Alexander Keiller, but rather a complex undertaking to decide where it ends. To many people the name of my subject means little save an association with marmalade and confectionery, yet his life was filled with many passions that his fortune allowed him to indulge.

His influence in many aspects of archaeology during the 1920s and 1930s was immensely significant in the decades to follow, and the excavations on Windmill Hill near Avebury, Wiltshire were a major step in the understanding of the British Neolithic period.

This was by no means his only contribution to the archaeological world. His vast funds enabled him to sponsor younger archaeologists, such as W. E. V . Young and Stuart Piggott, giving them a first foothold on the difficult ascent in their chosen profession. Keiller's interest in photography became integrated with his excavation work, leaving us with a meticulously detailed record of each stage in the excavations he undertook, much as one would expect to see on any current archaeological dig in progress. *Wessex from the Air*, a volume which brought to the fore the previously unexplored advantages of aerial photography in plotting and identifying archaeological sites, owes its conception solely to Keiller, who with O.G.S. Crawford as a guide and willing partner was able to implement his knowledge of both flying and photography during the course of the project.

Archaeology was not his only lasting interest in life, although it was perhaps the most predominant. He had a love of cars, which he was able to pursue by collecting just about anything that money could buy. His wealth also enabled him to finance a motor company — Sizaire-Berwick — in 1913, and here he learned draughtsmanship as an engineer, a skill which would stand him in good stead in the years to come.

He was an accomplished skier, specialising in ski-jumping and *langlauf,* and in 1932 he was President of the Ski Club of Great Britain. As a result of his

1

knowledge he was called upon to judge so many competitions and preside over so many councils during his winter stays in St Moritz, that often in later years he proclaimed he found precious little time to ski.

Other lasting passions included the study of witchcraft, most especially the sixteenth-century witch trials in Aberdeenshire, and criminology. The latter was pursued in depth when he served in the Special Constabulary from 1939-45 in Wiltshire, and he was able to put his considerable knowledge of the subject to good use. He had more than a passing interest in sexual techniques and rituals, and had an extensive collection of books on various related matters, both ancient and modern. Following his death, some of his surviving correspondence was deemed so scandalous that it was burned, and further letters were thrown from Westminster Bridge. In spite of four wives, who ran almost in immediate succession, he had a string of mistresses, and seemed to be ever restless, always searching for something which eluded him. Whether this was a subconscious desire to produce an heir, we cannot say, although he died without ever fathering any children. His restlessness was not quelled until he met his last wife, Gabrielle, with whom he settled down at the age of fifty nine to enjoy the remaining years of his life.

As you turn the pages and unfold the chapters of his life, be assured that you will be reading the history of a remarkable, enigmatic and at times mysterious individual. He was a man who lived life to the full, pursuing everything to the bounds of his abilities and embracing it with an abundance of enthusiasm and vigour.

I hope that this book does him justice.

2
TURNING MARMALADE INTO MONEY

THE KEILLER FAMILY has its roots planted firmly in the rich soil of Dundee, having been traced back as far as George Keler of Dundee, 1605.[1] (There are many variations on the spelling of Keiller — Keler, Killor and Keillor to list but a few). Thenceforth it branches out to many divides which through the ages have borne some remarkable fruit, the most notable of course being the original 'James Keiller' who founded the company in 1797, and his mother Janet Mathewson. They were the people who paved the way to untold wealth, and world-wide fame for the name of Keiller in future generations.

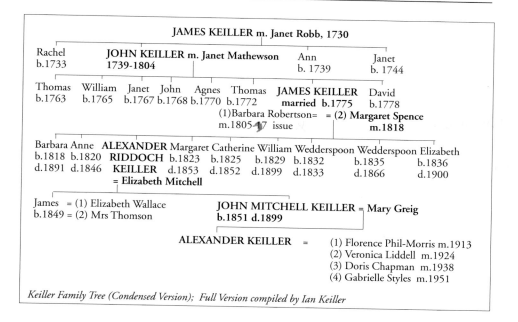

Keiller Family Tree (Condensed Version); Full Version compiled by Ian Keiller

The word 'marmalat' originally comes from the Portuguese marmelo, meaning 'quince'. There are many stories regarding the origins of marmalade, with references as far back as Henry VIII, and Mary Queen of Scots, but there is little doubt that on a commercial footing, and in association with oranges, the story begins in Dundee with the Keiller family. Somewhere in the mists of time and poetic licence the matter has become woven into legend, but we must believe that the seeds of truth remain.

John Keiller[2] was born in 1737, son of James Keiller and Janet (née Robb). He grew up to be a tailor, and a burgess of Dundee. In 1762 he married Janet Mathewson, and some time following this event, the traditional family recipe for making marmalade was passed on to 'the young Mrs Keiller' by the previous generation.

Here is where the legend goes off at a tangent, muddling Janets and Jameses, and wringing its hands with glee as it tells of '... a ship laden with Seville oranges sailing into port at Dundee, with no buyer for her cargo. An impulsive gesture by a member of the Keiller family gave Janet the opportunity to try out her marmalade recipe with a different fruit....'.

Whatever the truth of the matter — and a ship from Spain roaming the high seas with a cargo of oranges seems improbable — somewhere along the line, between 1762 and 1797, the making of marmalade with oranges rather than quinces was perfected by the Keillers, and production began.

Fig. 1. Janet Mathewson, Dundee *P. Keiller*

John and Janet had eight children, but it was their son James (1775-1839) whose name spearheaded the company. At the outset in 1797, James was a bachelor, and thus the '& Sons' would not have been added until later.

A factory was built in Dundee, which in itself was an ideal location, being close to a sugar refinery and the River Tay. The first tentative offering to the public was a 'chip' marmalade, which incorporated shredded peel rather than the pulped peel that was favoured in the English dessert. The invention of the mechanical peel cutter is attributed to a Wedderspoon Keiller, and there are several possible candidates of this name — sons, cousins, brother-in-law. Whoever it was, let us accept that it was a close family member.

Interest in the preserve spread beyond the boundaries of Dundee to Edinburgh, where recipes began to appear in cookery books published there. A distinctive white pottery jar was designed, and the name of the product adapted to emphasise its own special qualities. Keiller's Orange Marmalade was in demand almost as soon as it first reached the market, and owing to its popularity as a delicacy

4

it became a most desirable addition to every kitchen pantry.

James Keiller's first wife, Barbara Robertson (1789-1817) died at the age of twenty eight, having borne seven children, but it was the offspring of the second marriage to Margaret Spence (1800-1850), who were to continue the running and expansion of the company. Following James' death in 1839, Margaret took over the company until her sons attained their majority. Of her eight surviving children, only three were boys. Alexander was the eldest at 18 years, with William 10 years and Wedderspoon only 3 years old.

When he reached the age of twenty-one in 1842, Alexander took his place in the company, and the business continued to flourish. Later, in 1857, a new factory was built on the island of Guernsey to bypass sugar duties imposed by the Government. This astute business decision gave the Keillers a keener edge on their competitors, for there was no restriction on the importing of marmalade or confectionery from the island. This new branch was run by Wedderspoon, who had that same year attained his majority.

In March of 1859, a fire started in the engine room of the Dundee factory, causing widespread damage. Following this the plant was updated, and more modern preserving techniques were able to be introduced.

Following the repeal on sugar duties in 1874, a decision to move the Guernsey production to mainland Britain brought about the construction of a purpose-built factory at Silvertown in London. In 1879 'Tay Wharf' was opened with William Keiller in control. William had taken over the running of the Guernsey factory following the death of his younger brother Wedderspoon in 1866. Most of the employees from Guernsey were also relocated with the company. Other sugar products such as candied peel and jujubes had been introduced by the firm to the general market, and proved a big success, although marmalade was by far the largest source of income.

William's brother Alexander, who had remained in Dundee with the firm, married Elizabeth Mitchell on 14 November 1848. They had a son James the following year, and on New Year's Day in 1851 they had another boy whom they named John Mitchell Keiller. John[3] was educated at Dundee High School and from there went on to Edinburgh University. He left before graduating, and spent two years on the Continent learning both French and German. On returning home he entered the family business as an assistant to his father, who was then head of the company. His older brother James also worked for the firm during this period, but had not been offered a partnership when he attained his majority, and neither was he given the opportunity when his sibling John reached this stage in 1872. John became a full partner in the company at the age of twenty-one, but James was seemingly ostracised for behaviour both at work and socially that his father deemed unsuitable.

Five years after John took up his position in the company, his father died. This left him to assume the duties of a principal of the company, which was the largest of its kind in the country. He took on the challenge with enthusiasm, and although he did not enlarge the range of products on the market, he was keen to promote them across the world '..ever on the alert to widen the industry by opening up new markets..'.[4] 'The Only Prize Medal for Marmalade, London 1862', and the 'Grand Medal of Merit, Vienna 1873', which were proudly displayed on the old pottery marmalade jars, were boosted by further awards from Australia, India and South Africa.[5]

Fig. 2. John Mitchell Keiller, father of Alexander Keiller
Dundee County Council Central Library

3
SON AND HEIR

ON FEBRUARY 5th 1884, John had married Mary Greig, who came from a well known and esteemed Dundee medical family. The Greigs had been surgeons for generations as far back as the chirurgeon-barber days, and even in some instances surgeons on whaling ships. Mary's brother David M. Greig was eventu-

Fig. 3. Binrock House, Dundee. Birthplace of Alexander, 1889 *Sharon Darrall*

ally conservator of the College of Surgeons Museum in Edinburgh after many years following in the footsteps of his ancestors.[6]

The newly married couple lived at Binrock House in Dundee, a large house with sprawling gardens that overlooked the River Tay. In 1886 John bought the Morven and Gairnside portion of the Marquess of Huntly's estates near Ballater in Aberdeenshire, an area of some 10,000 acres, and just eight miles from Balmoral Castle. The land, which was highly priced because of the excellent shooting available, was sold with all shooting and fishing rights, and five tenanted farms. Queen Victoria herself had shown some interest when the estate was put up for sale, but the initial price of £50,000 was deemed too high. Morven Hill, which stands at an elevation of 2,862ft /872m, stands on the estate and was a favourite excursion for the queen when she was residing at nearby Balmoral.[7]

Lord Byron, who had spent childhood vacations in the area, was to write later:

> 'When I roved, a young Highlander, o'er the dark heath,
> And climbed thy steep summit, O Morven, of snow,
> To gaze on the torrents that thundered beneath,
> Or the mist of thy tempest that thundered below...'

A Scottish newspaper reported that in purchasing the estate, which included one of the best grouse moors in Aberdeenshire, John Mitchell Keiller had demonstrated fully the power of marmalade.[8]

7

To begin with, during the shooting season, the family would spend their time at the Morven Lodge, but this building was impractical when it came to housing an extensive shooting party. It was also too far from the railway station at Ballater. John Keiller decided to build a mansion on the estate, with no expense spared, to supplement his town residence in Dundee. The mansion was not to be built of granite, as was every other building in the Ballater area, but of red sandstone from his home county of Fife. The huge blocks had to be transported by rail to Ballater and then hauled up to the chosen site on carts. The house, when it was built, was named 'Invercauld', and even today the original facade is as striking in colour as it must have been over a hundred years ago when it was built.

Fig. 4. Invercauld at Morven, Aberdeenshire (now the Stakis Balmoral Hotel) *Author*

Peter de Savory ?

John Keiller was a generous patron in all areas, and deemed it important to share certain aspects of his wealth with his home town of Dundee. In 1887, to celebrate the Jubilee, he donated over 3,000 books to the Dundee Free Library, and cleared the somewhat extensive debts of the Albert Institute, allowing the expansion of the Galleries there. From time to time he loaned parts of his considerable art collection, which included valuable works by artists such as Constable and Turner, to local exhibitions. He was also a Justice of the Peace for Forfarshire and the County and City of Dundee.[9]

On December 1st 1889, a son was born to Mary and John Keiller at their home in Dundee. He was to be their only child, and heir to the great marmalade fortune. They named him Alexander.

When his son was four years old, John Mitchell Keiller gave up his residence in Dundee, as well as his interest in the family business, owing to health problems. 'James Keiller & Sons' became a limited liability company with John Mitchell Keiller as Chairman. Following the sale of Binrock House in Dundee, he moved to 13 Hyde Park Gardens in London with his family,[10] although for at least a part of every summer they travelled to Scotland to enjoy the bracing airs of the Deeside Highlands at their home in Morven.

After retiring from both the business and public life in 1893, John Keiller spent an increasing amount of time aboard his yacht, sailing to warmer climates in an effort to alleviate his health problems. For a young Alexander, his father must have seemed but a distant figure of authority who made occasional appearances. Following his first term at Hazelwood Preparatory School at Limpsfield in Surrey in Autumn 1898, Alexander returned home to find that his father had already set sail for Madeira aboard his 568-ton steam yacht *The Erl King*. He spent Christmas at home with his mother.

In late December, John Mitchell Keiller set sail on the final leg of his journey from Madeira bound for the West Indies, accompanied by his private secretary and a young doctor. This was to be his final voyage. On January 2nd 1899, the day after his forty-ninth birthday he died at sea, leaving his widow Mary, and his son Alexander who was nine years old. The value of his estate was estimated at just under half a million pounds, which at today's levels would have made him a multi-millionaire.

Later that year, the factory in Tay Wharf, London, was seriously damaged by fire, and in May 1900, the Dundee plant was entirely destroyed by a fire which originated in an explosion in the refrigerating machine of the chocolate department. In this instance, due to the measures taken to secure the safety of the staff, the fire was given sufficient time to take hold. One of the local papers, which dedicated several pages to reporting on the fire, described '... Four large buildings, with only the four walls standing, filled with a burning fiery mass of debris ... and slowly but surely the wind was carrying the flames towards a great magazine in which were stored hundreds of tons of sugar ...'.[11] The sugar was saved by a stout gable wall and the 'unremitting exertions' of the firemen, but it was too late to save the factory. In a matter of hours, over £70,000 of damage was caused (no small sum at that time), and the several hundred employees were thrown idle until the completion of the new replacement plant. Thankfully the premises were insured, and a new plant was built.

Fig. 5. Newspaper article reporting the great fire at the Keiller Factory in Dundee, May 1900
(© D.C. Thomson and Co. Ltd.)

By 1905 the company had recovered sufficiently to demand the whole of the Minor Hall for the Grocer's Exhibition at the Agricultural Hall in Islington, London. This area of approximately 12,000 square feet was deemed necessary in order to give their products adequate presentation. Records state that no fewer than sixty-three thousand preserve packages were displayed.

At this time, Dundee Marmalade had gained such popularity that it was said if every 1lb jar sold by just one company in a year was stood in a tightly packed line, then that line would stretch from Dundee to London, a distance of 422 miles.

In 1940, during the first large-scale air raid on London in World War II, the Silvertown factory, covering almost seven acres, was completely destroyed. When the war ended, a new factory was built at Maryfield on the outskirts of Dundee. At the same time improvements were made to the Albert Square factory (now dedicated to the manu-

facture of confectionery, especially butterscotch), with the new Maryfield site used en-
tirely for Marmalade, and the production of Toblerone chocolate. The business contin-
ued to expand, and eventually passed out of family hands. Production moved away
from Dundee, although the name 'James Keiller & Sons' remains to this day.

4
YOUNG ALEXANDER

AFTER THE DEATH of his father, Alexander continued with his studies at
Hazelwood Prep until 1903. An entry in the school magazine 'list of leavers' in
August of that year notes '... A.Keiller goes to Eton. He has not been able to take a
prominent part in the field, but has been a great help on the stage ...'.[12]

Fig. 6. Keiller at Eton *WA&NHS Library, Devizes*

11

At Eton, Keiller's housemaster was John Montague Hare. Houses at Eton are known by the name of the master, and not the building. He was at Eton from Michaelmas 1903 until Summer 1907. He gained no prizes, awards or scholarships, and seems only to have reached the middle ranks of the school in academic achievement. However, he was a Private in the 'Eton Rifles'.[13] This Corps was founded in 1860 as the 'Eton College Rifle Volunteers'. Over the following decades it was attached to the First Buckingham and then the Oxford Light Infantry, but when Keiller was enrolled in September 1905 it was known as the 2nd Bucks (Eton College) Volunteer Rifle Corps. During his time in the Corps, he would have taken part in rifle practice, drills, field days and compulsory annual camp. Doubtless this training proved useful in the not too distant future when he was at Ypres, and elsewhere, during the Great War.

Fig. 7. Keiller at Morven, early 1900s   *WA&NHS Library, Devizes*

In January of 1907, when Alexander was only just turned seventeen, his mother died in Nice, France. Perhaps it was due to this tragedy that he left Eton in the summer of that year. His uncle became his guardian, and the family fortune, which was Alexander's alone now, was put into trust until he attained his majority.

Whilst on the family estates at Morven, during holidays and school exeats he had become interested in local archaeological sites, most specifically recumbent stone circles,[14] and began to make a record of what he saw. Here were the first steps towards an interest which would influence his life for many years to follow. It is likely, since there were few field archaeologists active in North East Scotland during this time, that Keiller gleaned some knowledge of his subject from Dr William Douglas Simpson, who became a prominent figure in Scottish archaeology fairly early in his career.[15]

Towards the close of 1910, on his twenty-first birthday, Keiller came into his inheritance and became actively involved in the family business. Initially he declined the offer of becoming a Director, preferring to take a back seat and allow his uncle, John Keiller Greig, to represent him at Board meetings. In 1911 Keiller allocated enough shares in the company to his uncle to allow him to become a Director as Keiller's representative. He also began to accumulate yet further shares for himself. In order to assist the company during a temporary cashflow difficulty he offered to buy up shares in one of the overseas branches at Tangermunde, near Berlin in Germany, thus increasing his stockholding. His involvement in the business increased marginally, with the occasional attendance of Annual Directors Board Meetings, which seemed to have been convened most often to award Directors salaries and bonuses.[16] Quite often though, owing to these meetings being convened in the winter months, there was a letter of apology from Keiller at St Moritz, where he was obviously trying to escape the pressures of executive stress.[17]

5
A TIME OF CHANGE — 1913

KEILLER'S MILITARY RECORD states that he was in the '7th Gordon Highlanders' from May 1911 until October 1913, although there is no evidence to suggest active service during this period. However, Keiller himself mentions in a letter that shortly before the outbreak of World War One he resigned his commission, and in 1909 during the Panther-Agadir incident he was a Brigade machine gun officer.[17a]

In January 1913, Keiller competed in his first British Ski event in St Moritz, winning the Ski Club of Great Britain cup for a jump on the Julierschanze of 84ft 6in / 25.7m. In Spring of the same year, he married his first wife, Florence Phil-Morris, at the Old Church, Chelsea in London, and they took up residence at his house in Hyde Park Gardens, spending the Summer and Christmas at Morven. They spent the first three years of their marriage moving between London, Scotland, and a house at the Rue de la Chaise in Paris.[18]

6
FLORENCE PHIL-MORRIS

FLORENCE WAS SEVEN YEARS OLDER than Keiller. On her marriage certificate she stated her age as twenty five when she was in truth almost thirty. She was born in 1883, as Florence Marian Morris, daughter of Philip Richard Morris, an award-winning artist of the Royal Academy, and Catherine Serjeantson, the widowed daughter of a 'Gentleman'. Her mother died of exhaustive phthisis seemingly in reduced circumstances working as a laundress, when Florence was seventeen. Her father died two years later in 1902, having exhibited at the RA and elsewhere until the year before his death.[19]

As well as reducing her age, the resourceful Florence also altered her name. Her father signed many of his paintings 'Phil Morris', and this Florence adopted as a hyphenated surname, whilst adding a flourish to her middle name making it 'Marianne'.

The marriage was not to last, and it has been suggested that Florence married him for his money, although there is no evidence to support this. In late summer of 1915, Keiller left his wife without any explanation, and ignored her pleas for him to return. He did, however, contribute towards her support, and still classed himself as married on the military records which survive from the War.

On the marriage certificate Keiller lists his profession as 'Motor Agent'. Two weeks after the wedding, in June of 1913 the company 'Sizaire-Berwick (France) Limited' was registered, with Keiller as a Director and main investor. He already at that time had a love of cars, and his inheritance gave him the opportunity to play a prominent part in the development and manufacture of this new motor vehicle.

7
THE RISE AND FALL OF THE SIZAIRE-BERWICK

DURING THE FIRST DECADE of the 1900s, Maurice and Georges Sizaire, along with their friend and colleague Louis Naudin, had designed and produced a moderately priced sports car. It was known as the Sizaire-Naudin, and had been continually successful, winning both the 1906 Coupe de Voiturettes in France and the 185 mile 'Voiturette Sicilian Cup race' over the Long Madonie circuit in

1907. However, after a disappointing racing season with 4-cylinder cars in 1912, the three men turned their attention to improving the design of passenger vehicles.

At around this time in London, a used car dealer named F. W. Berwick was taking stock of his flourishing empire and concluded that the moment had come for him to venture into the business of car manufacture.

A motoring journalist by the name of W. F. Bradley, who had known the Sizaire brothers for many years, introduced them to Berwick, and thus the idea of the Sizaire-Berwick was born. All they needed was a wealthy backer, which they found — again through Bradley — in the form of an enthusiastic Alexander Keiller.

The prototype was built, designed to be a 20hp scaled down visual replica of the 40/50hp Rolls-Royce Silver Ghost with a smooth running 4-cylinder engine as opposed to the 6-cylinder engine of the Rolls-Royce. It underwent exhaustive testing both at Brooklands and on the open roads. A wager of £25 between Berwick and Keiller gave the car its first long run. Keiller said that the prototype could not travel from London to Edinburgh in less than twelve hours, unlike his own 'Prince Henry' Austro Daimler which often made the journey in that time.

Berwick took up the challenge, and at 7.30 one mist-shrouded morning the two seater Sizaire-Berwick, having rough mock-up bodywork but without windscreen or wings, rolled out of Hyde Park and raced north on the open road. Mud spattered and road weary, it drew up outside the Central Hotel in Edinburgh, some 400 miles away from the starting point, at 6.20 the same evening. Covering such a distance in less than twelve hours was quite a spectacular achievement in 1912, and Keiller gladly conceded.[20] Keiller and Berwick became friends during that period, and Berwick's son was named John Alexander for Keiller, who was appointed his godfather.

THE COMPANY 'SIZAIRE-BERWICK (FRANCE) LTD' was registered on June 13th 1913. Home offices were at 18 Berkeley Street in London, not far from Keiller's home, with the factory being at 43, rue Louis Blanc in Courbevoie on the outskirts of Paris. The chassis were built at the factory with 20 per cent of production earmarked for the French market. The remainder were driven to the port in batches of three, being road tested en route by Jack Waters, who was better known later as Jack Warner of 'Dixon of Dock Green'. From the port they were shipped to a small assembly plant in Highgate, London where the majority were fitted with coachwork for the British market, which involved a considerable increase in price over the standard Sizaire-Berwick tourer.

The 20hp Sizaire-Berwick made its public debut in Paris during October 1913 although cars may have been sold before this launch from the Berkeley Street

Fig. 8. Keiller's own Sizaire-Berwick, which was used by him as a staff car during the 1914-18 war
NMM Library, Beaulieu

showrooms in London. The remarkable appearance of this chic Rolls-Royce lookalike, which benefitted from better fuel economy, lower taxation and smoother performance than its counterpart, secured many orders at the Paris show with hard cash. The French magazine *La Vie Automobile* described it as the chassis of a true luxury car.[21]

The small factory began to turn out cars at an average of five per week until the end of June 1914. The chassis price was £475, with a complete car ranging from £745 - £860 depending upon individual specifications. Although some 130 units were made, supply never quite caught up with demand. One of the last chassis to be shipped over to London in August before the outbreak of war was fitted out as an armoured car for the Royal Naval Air Service, and several tourers were held by the R.N.A.S. as staff cars, one such car being used by Keiller during the Great War. This car was presented to the National Motor Museum at Beaulieu by his widow in June 1959, having been restored and run successfully by J G Hutt of Newbury. This typical 1914 20hp Sizaire-Berwick, registration number SB-785 is a five-seater tourer with cream paintwork on an aluminium body. It has a capacity of 4060cc and is four cylinder. An interesting added feature is that the front seat folds down to make a bed.[22] A Scottish newspaper reported in 1988 that the car had served with Keiller during the Great War on the Western Front, suffering slight damage from machine gun fire which can still be seen on the bonnet today.[23]

One of the cars which had remained on the Continent was used throughout the war for the personal transport of the former President of France, Raymond Poincaré. This reflected the level of prestige which Sizaire-Berwick had achieved in a matter of only months, and was ultimately confirmed by Poincaré's choice of driver — an army sergeant better known as Georges Sizaire.

During the war years, the factory was dedicated to wartime production. This may have been partly through the influence of Keiller, who joined the Royal Naval Volunteer Reserve in October 1914 and was sent for 'Special Service' in the entirely new division of 'Armoured Cars'.[24]

The concept of armoured cars was relatively new in this period, but the potential advantage had been noticed and acted upon by Charles Rumney Sampson,[24a] and in September 1914 a request was made by the Controller of the Admiralty Air Department, Commander Murray Sueter, to his superior Winston Churchill, for sixty fighting cars. Churchill seized this opportunity to become involved in the land war, which was not strictly R.N.A.S. business, and the request was accepted. The first designs implemented had many flaws, and as new design features were introduced to rectify these problems, the vehicles in service began to differ extensively in the early days as the search for perfection continued. Once the

Fig. 9. Sizaire-Berwick's prototype 'Wind-wagon' at the R.N.A.S. test ground, circa 1915
Tank Museum, Bovington

creases were ironed out, large-scale production began in earnest.[25]

When the heavy armoured vehicles were used in desert conditions, they would become bogged down in the soft sand and soon lose their traction, thus rendering them both inoperable and vulnerable to attack. An alternative method of propulsion was designed.

This was built in London as a mock up on a Sizaire-Berwick chassis, and fitted with a 110hp Sunbeam aircraft engine at the rear which drove a four-bladed airscrew. This was supposed literally to blow the car along if it became stuck in the sand. Owing to the amount of space taken by the engine, little room remained for the fighting compartment. A slope-fronted cab with enough room for a driver and front facing gunner was built in mild steel. Unfortunately it did not develop beyond the prototype stage. A shortage of aircraft engines made their use as auxiliary power units for armoured cars impossible.

Other armoured vehicles were constructed on chassis of other makes, such as Leyland, including machine gun and searchlight lorries, travelling photographic dark rooms and telephone exchanges, and living wagons for crews, these mainly being built on heavy Leyland chassis.

In 1915 F. W. Berwick purchased a site at Park Royal in North London, and began work on a factory which would ultimately cover 16 acres, where 110hp Le Rhone engines and planes would be constructed, including DH(de Havilland)4, DH9, DH9A and DH10 twin engined bombers. The DH4 2 seater fighter/bombers were manufactured at a cost of £1200 excluding the cost of their engines, which ranged from 200hp liquid cooled BHP in-line engines to later 375hp Rolls-Royce Eagle VIII's of similar configuration.

These contracts proved to be most profitable, as well as being conducive towards the war effort, and when the War ended, Berwick was affluent and eager enough to resume production of the Sizaire-Berwick on a far grander scale, owing to his newly equipped Park Royal factory.

The Sizaire brothers moved to London with their draughtsmen, and made some alterations to the original design. Rolls Royce in the meantime had not been at all happy with the new company's almost perfect reproduction of its famous radiator, and because Sizaire-Berwick was a British company rather than purely French, steps were taken to put a stop to this. The modified radiator was not a success, and the car lost much of its aesthetic appeal.

To make matters worse Keiller had employed one of his relatives in the company to look after his interests. The uncle, who had previously worked in a company producing steam rollers, demanded that the chassis be thickened and reinforced for solidity. This proved to be disastrous. A thousand components were ordered to these new specifications without the most basic prototype having been built. By the time a problem came to light it was too late, and Sizaire's original concept of a light simple chassis was brought to an abrupt halt by a car which was 'too heavy to get out of its own way'.[25a] This was by no way the only reason for the decline of the company, but must certainly have been a contributor.

Only 200 cars were made after the war before the British company went into the hands of the Official Receiver. The French company was bought by an American named Burke in 1919. A few of the remaining British built postwar Sizaire-Berwicks were sold from a fashionable new showroom at Champs Elysees in Paris. Maurice Sizaire's services were retained, and he designed a new chassis called the 4RI which was a revolutionary idea in automotive engineering, and proved a great success. For the British company however, time had run out long before, and Keiller was left to dwell upon the consequences of his mistake.[26]

8
OFFICER CL ASS

KEILLER'S MILITARY CAREER during the Great War was varied. He joined up on October 9th 1914 as a Temporary Lieutenant in the R.N.V.R., and was sent for 'Special Service' with *HMS Pembroke*, which was an official name for officer postings at a variety of shore establishments. By December he was under 'Special Service' with the R.N.A.S., alongside many names now associated with the development of armoured cars. His civilian occupation is listed as 'Motor Engineer' which may suggest why he was chosen for the new department formed to develop the armoured car. In April of 1915 he went over to France, where he remained until he was invalided out.[26a]

Here, his personal account of his activities differs slightly from official records. In a letter to Awdry in 1938 he claims that he 'got back [to England] and joined another Squadron', though records state that at the end of June 1915 he was promoted to Temporary Acting Flight Lieutenant (still with Armoured Cars) and transferred to Chingford,[27] a small 'second class landing ground' north of London which had only two months previously become the main training station for R.N.A.S. pilots. At Chingford he was 'second-in-command of an instructional school with a ship's company of 650, and officers under instruction to the number of 115'.[27a]

A month after his transfer it was reported that Keiller had 'damaged' a Bristol Box-kite Biplane (No 943) which had arrived at Chingford in May for completion. The damage is not listed, but he did not crash the plane, as it would have been reported as such. Indeed, the plane in question was crashed only a week later by a

Fig. 10. Flight Lieutenant Alexander Keiller, R.N.A.S. *RAF Museum Hendon*

Sub Lieutenant Morgan, repaired, and finally deleted from service in October the same year.[28]

Still with the Armoured Car Division, on 27th November Keiller obtained his Aviator's Certificate, granted by the Royal Aero Club of the United Kingdom. His test was taken at Chingford in an Avro Biplane. At this time there was no distinct military aviation training, and R.N.A.S. pilots qualified in the same way as civilians. A month after obtaining his pilot's licence Keiller was assessed and reported unfit for service, and on 24th January 1916 his commission was terminated owing to his being 'physically unfit'.[29]

What the cause of his medical problem was we do not know, but in 1917, at the height of the War, he managed 'by some means best known to himself" to get out to St Moritz for five days to do some skiing.[30]

His military career did not end with the R.N.V.R., and on 29th July 1918 he joined the Air Ministry as a Temporary Lieutenant. Two months later he was appointed as Staff Officer 3rd class (this probably refers to his salary grade) with the Deputy Directorate of Air Intelligence, and made a Temporary Captain, reporting to Major Erskine Childers D.S.C.[31]

His varied career in both Services during the Great War took him to many places, as far afield as Ypres in France, and Riga in Russia. He had also spent some time on the Italian Front, and subsequently 'entertained the poorest opinion of Italian military prowess'.[32]

He remained with Air Intelligence until April 1919, when he was transferred to the Unemployed list and granted Honorary Rank of Captain.

9
THE EARLY 1920s

KEILLER'S ASSOCIATION with the family business had not diminished during the War Years, and another time of change for him was 1918. In March of that year, he elected to sell all of his shares in the company, including those inherited from his father, and also the 100 shares held by his uncle, John Keiller Greig. These shares were bought up in the main by other Directors in the company, as well as outsiders.[33] Thus his involvement with his family business ceased, and with the considerable fortune there accrued, he was free to do as he chose.

This fresh start prompted him to apply for a divorce from Florence, with whom he had not lived for almost three years. He sent her a receipt from a London Hotel stating that a 'Mr & Mrs Keiller' had spent the night there. As Florence was residing in Cornwall at the time, she knew this to be an admission of adultery, and agreed to divorce him on those grounds. The divorce proceedings took place in Scotland, with Keiller claiming Scottish domicile, where he was able to escape the marital bonds for a modest settlement of £50 plus court costs.[34] Florence spent some years in Cornwall, at a little cottage in Perranuthnoe near Penzance, before moving to Berkshire.[35] She died in France the same year as Keiller died, without ever having remarried. Perhaps it had been love after all.

10
WITCHCRAFT AND DEMONS

ONE OF KEILLER'S INTERESTS throughout his life was witchcraft, most specifically sixteenth-century witchcraft in Scotland. In 1922 he had an article published in *Folklore* entitled 'Witchcraft in Scotland'. He acquired an extensive and varied selection of volumes for his library in 1922, dating back as far as 1452, which he kept in a section entitled Witchcraft, Demonology and Devil-lore'.[36]

He wrote an article later published in *Folklore* entitled 'The Personnel of Aberdeenshire Witchcraft Covens in the Years 1596-7',[37] which was privately reprinted in the form of a small book. This was a technical work which must have required a considerable amount of research, and goes into obsessive detail regarding relationships of the women involved and the conclusions of their individual trials in the sixteenth century. The essay quite openly contradicts evidence previously put forward by an eminent specialist, Margaret Murray, in 'The Witch Cult in Western Europe',[38] and Keiller states at the start of his work that it is his desire to criticise Miss Murray. In her book, Murray had, to support her own theory, created from 16th-century sources covens of thirteen. It must be remembered that before Murray's book was published in 1921 there had been no extensive study of unpublished data on this subject, and therefore the volume was greeted with critical acclaim as a pioneering work. Keiller greeted it with scepticism, and spent a vast amount of time poring over the same sources as Murray, but came up with entirely different conclusions. Even limited investigation showed that many of the women on trial must have been solitary individuals, and not at all part of a coven. Often names, locations and dates did not correlate. Keiller picked up on these discrepancies, and the product of his exhaustive research was published in the article previously mentioned. It was not until the 1970s that widely read authors such as Keith Thomas and Norman Cohn published equally critical assessments of Murray's book as discussed in Ronald Hutton's *Pagan Religions of the British Isles*, and it was accepted that she had been wrong. Half a century earlier, Keiller had come to the same conclusions.

He continued to collect books to add to his library, including a copy of the *L'Inconstance des Demons* which had belonged to the Bishop of Aush in the early seventeenth century. He considered this volume a classic on Witchcraft in the Basque country, and as late as 1951 he was contemplating the possibility of translating the work into both English and modern French in order to publish it in the form of a limited edition.

This treasured book was protected by an outer casing of brown calf leather which encased the original bindings. Many of the books in Keiller's extensive personal library were bound in this fashion, a foible of his which stemmed from his desire for order and uniformity.

In a letter in 1930, Keiller states that his study of Witchcraft was somewhat abruptly abandoned in favour of the more pressing needs of his professional work as regards Prehistoric Archaeology. He adds, 'Some ten years ago I light-heartedly commenced a complete report, with detailed surveys, of the Megalithic Monuments of Aberdeenshire and Kincardineshire, this work subsequently enlarged to take in the Megalithic Monuments of North-East Scotland ...'.[39]

And so it was Archaeology that usurped the subject of Witchcraft, as like a petulant puppy it demanded more time than any other interest, winning Keiller over with mute appeal but finding in him a shrewd master.

He did not wholly abandon the subject of Witchcraft, and in the 1930s, one Halloween night found him leading a small group of associates out into the garden of the Manor at Avebury. He carried before him a phallic symbol, and bowing three times before the Statue of Pan, he chanted 'witchlike' incantations. His secretary at that time, Mrs Sorel-Taylour, was present but did not take this strange behaviour seriously.[40]

11
FIRST CONTACT

IN 1920, O. G. S. Crawford was appointed as the first Archaeological Officer for the Ordnance Survey, where he made his chief objective the construction of an accurate series of Period maps. To this end he was given the task of sifting through the 'chaotic mixture of antiquarianism and speculation that disfigured the OS maps'[41] such as 'druidic altars'. Crawford had also spent some years in the Royal Flying Corps during the War, which had in turn sparked an interest in aerial surveying, a subject with close associations with his new post.

Two years after his appointment, following an aerial reconnaissance mission by the Royal Air Force, several curious marks were noticed on the photographs taken above Hampshire. These photos were passed on to the Ordnance Survey where they finally filtered down to Crawford, who was able to recognise and map out what proved to be a Celtic field system near Winchester.

This example and others were described by Crawford at a lecture given to the Royal Geographical Society on March 12 1922. As a result of the lecture, the Sunday press became interested. Crawford contributed an article to *The Sunday Observer*[42] the following year, and also a paper entitled 'Air Survey and Archaeology' which was read to the Royal Geographical society and subsequently published. His article in *The Sunday Observer* produced a response from no less than Alexander Keiller, who offered to undertake and finance the air reconnaissance of a large number of archaeological sites in Wessex.

During the summer of 1923, other events began to unfold which sealed the fate of Avebury in Wiltshire for decades to follow. The Marconi wireless company announced that they were to erect a radio mast on Windmill Hill, a prehistoric earthwork one mile north-west of Avebury village and stone circle. In 1922, on this hitherto neglected site nestled amidst the rolling Wiltshire downs, the Reverend Kendall of Winterbourne Monkton, who had for many years collected flints from the Avebury area, came across some sherds of pottery during his trial excavation of one of the ditches at Windmill Hill. Kendall had first cut a section into the earthwork in 1899 for archaeological examination, but it was the discovery of the pottery that sparked interest further afield.[43]

These finds were brought to the attention of Crawford (whose initial interest in archaeology had developed when he attended public school in nearby Marlborough as a boy), and proved to be Neolithic. When Crawford visited the site to plot the location of the finds, he was also able to identify the inner and middle ditches of the Windmill Hill site, as well as the outer ditch where the finds had been made.

Despite assurances to the local archaeological society by Marconi that no intentional damage would be done to the site, Crawford was horrified at the prospect, and launched a campaign to have the project abandoned. Keiller joined his crusade, and was a prominent ally working tirelessly to gain the support of many leading archaeologists and the public, both through the media and his influential contacts. In September the project was cancelled, not officially due to the pressure of public support for Crawford's campaign, but rather because the Government was concerned that the high mast would be dangerous to flying.[44]

The Marconi proposal had, however, highlighted the problem of preservation with regard to archaeological sites such as Windmill Hill. Crawford had written to Keiller shortly before the cancellation of the Marconi project suggesting that sites of national importance should be in the hands of private owners such as Keiller in order to assure their continuing survival. Keiller deemed the plan 'a patriotic act which, if carried out by a few keen antiquaries could not but result, Marconi Co. or no Marconi Co., in a permanent advantage to archaeology'. [45] Here the seed of possibility was sown which would reap a great harvest of wealth in the years to come.

During the autumn of 1923 Keiller was busy with a variety of archaeological activities near his home in Morven, Scotland. He was fascinated by the recumbent type of stone circle which is predominant in North East Scotland, and set about collating the data he had gathered on this subject. Also, having at last obtained the permission of the Laird at neighbouring Dinnet and Kinnord, he was able to organise and direct a small excavation on the Laird's estate.[46]

He wrote to Crawford, who was at that time excavating near the famous monument of Stonehenge, saying that had he been in England for more than a couple of days during that period he would have been very tempted to offer his services 'in any sort of honorary capacity from light lorry driver upwards, purely

LETTERS TO THE EDITOR.

DANGER TO PREHISTORIC SITE.

Morven, near Ballater, Aberdeenshire,
August 12, 1923.

SIR,—The fact that a proverbially large proportion of Scotsmen are to a greater or less degree interested in antiquarian research renders me less diffident in begging you, through the medium of your journal, again to draw attention to the contemplated ruin of Avebury, the finest prehistoric site still existent in the world, by the proposed erection there of a private wireless station. Many of the masts will be in the parish of Avebury itself, while others (some said to be over 800 feet high) will disfigure the adjacent countryside, which, as many of your readers must know, represents an only partially explored treasure-land of archæological interest and value.

Perhaps an even more horrible side of the proposal is that a large number of houses are to be built in connection with the scheme just outside the village of Avebury itself. Even Tom Robinson, the leader of the vandals who, in the eighteenth century, destroyed so many of the mighty monoliths for the purpose of utilising the stone in the erection of trumpery cottages, could not have treated this greatest monument in Britain, or, for that matter, of its kind in the world, with greater disdain and indifference.

All too swiftly are the great prehistoric sites of Britain, whether in earth or stone, succumbing to the destructive, and too often utterly senseless, actions of ignorant farmers, and perhaps less ignorant, but thereby even more selfish, proprietors, or of rural authorities or commercial organisations. Must Avebury — Avebury the unique, the most marvellous of them all—suffer as has its most important rival, Stonehenge, around which barrows galore have been destroyed within the past few years alone, where the wonderful cursus is now barely discernible, whose very avenue, at the moment of fresh discoveries through the means of aerial photography, is threatened, while the actual circles themselves are dwarfed by an unsightly and unnecessary aerodrome, and disfigured by glaring advertisements for tea-rooms and such-like enticements for trippers.

The time left is short; on July 23rd the Postmaster-General stated that he hoped that the agreement with the Marconi Company would be signed "in a fortnight or a month." Will not those of your readers who are in sympathy with this appeal at the eleventh hour do all that they can to avert the impending catastrophe? If they will, then let them express their opinions publicly, let them appeal to their members of Parliament, let them do all in their power, and there is much that they can do, to preserve inviolate one of Britain's sacred treasures.—I am, &c.

ALEX. KEILLER, F.S.A. (Scot.)

Fig. 11. Keiller's letter to *The Scotsman* as part of the campaign to prevent the Marconi Company erecting a mast on Windmill Hill. *The Scotsman*

Fig. 12. Veronica Liddell, Keiller's second wife, photo taken around 1927
Alexander Keiller Museum, Avebury

for the privilege of being present on such a prestigious site'.[47] With a subsequent letter he sent a photograph of the Citroen Kegresse, a half-track vehicle which he had purchased earlier that year in Paris. We shall hear more of the Kegresse later on.

12
VERONICA

O N THE TWENTY-NINTH of February 1924, Keiller married his second wife Veronica Liddell. The marriage was solemnized in the Church of Our Lady of the Assumption in the District of St Martin, London, and was not attended by any family members.

The Liddell family home was at Sherfield Manor near Basingstoke in Hampshire. Veronica's father was a Justice of the Peace, and also enjoyed the title 'Lord of the Manor'.[48] Her sister Dorothy was rapidly gaining recognition as an experienced field archaeologist, and in later years directed her own excavations in Devon and Hampshire.

The newly married couple moved into Keiller's house in Charles Street, which had for several years been his 'bachelor's residence' during his brief spells in London. Veronica took a degree in Archaeology, and joined the local archaeological society. Initially this was to identify herself with Keiller's own interest, so that they had a common ground, but as she progressed she found the work fascinating, and concentrated on her own particular field of study, which was settlement.[49]

Preparations were already in hand for the imminent air reconnaissance survey of archaeological sites as proposed by Keiller the previous autumn, when Crawford learned through Kendall that part of Windmill Hill, a portion that included part of the earthwork, some Bronze Age Barrows and a 'prolific flint site', was up for sale. He wrote to Keiller expressing the view that Windmill Hill was one of the most interesting and important sites in the South of England, and possibly where the makers of Avebury had lived.[50]

The latter statement — now known to be inaccurate — was enough to tip the scales in Crawford's favour. Keiller showed the letter to Veronica, who was quite keen on the idea of purchasing the site, until she read that there was a possibility of excavating dwellings, whereupon she went 'completely mad' with enthusiasm. Keiller told Crawford 'she will take an interest in anything in earth or stone that has an archaeological interest in much the same way as I will be transiently interested in a Lake Village, but as soon as she gets near dwellings of any description, her enthusiasm is only rivalled by mine on discovering a recumbent stone *in situ* between its fellow stones somewhere in Aberdeenshire'.[51]

This reply was followed closely by a visit to the proposed acquisition, where Keiller noted that the primary impression he had carried away from Windmill Hill was an aesthetic rather than an archaeological one, since both he and Veronica agreed that seldom in England had they seen so beautiful an area.[52] Negotiations for the purchase proceeded shortly afterwards, a prelude to the commencement of excavation work.

It was around this time that Keiller and his wife had tea at the vicarage in Winterbourne Monkton with Kendall, who was pleased at the prospect of the imminent Windmill Hill purchase. Kendall made a gift of some of his Windmill Hill finds to Veronica, and these were taken back to London to be placed in a temporary collection room at Charles Street.

13
WESSEX FROM THE AIR

THE EARLY SUMMER MONTHS were, for Keiller, taken up intermittently by aerial photography with Crawford. With their headquarters at the Knoll Hotel in Andover and based at the nearby Weyhill Aerodrome, they flew several sorties during which over three hundred photographs were taken. The aeroplane, a DeHavilland, was piloted by Captain Gaskell. The photographs were taken with an Ica camera which was fitted in the bottom of the observer's cockpit, with the negative size being 10 by 15cm.[53]

Fifty plates were finally chosen, each of an ancient site in Wessex. Every site had to be visited and walked over, with Crawford making annotations on a matt print of each site in order to draw up explanatory diagrams to accompany the photograph. Much of the technical work was done during office hours at the Ordnance Survey. Crawford had not been made welcome at the OS, which had previously been the exclusive domain of the Royal Engineer Officers. Not only was he a civilian, but it was general consensus in those days that archaeology was a relatively unimportant contribution to the work of the OS. For these reasons his superiors were quite happy for him to work on 'Wessex', which was indirectly useful to them for correcting and completing maps, and kept him out of their hair.

Thus the foundation stones were laid for *Wessex from the Air*, to be built upon over the following years until the volume was published in 1928.

KEILLER WAS INVOLVED with almost every aspect of the publication, being most particular about the layout and content to such a degree that on occasion he would send several letters in one day to Mr Norrington, (who worked for the publishers Clarendon Press in Oxford), in order to emphasise each point individually. Despite Keiller's obsession with detail and the barrage of mail he inflicted upon Norrington, the two men became correspondents on a personal level following the publication, and were friends for many years thereafter.

There is no doubt that *Wessex from the Air* was a completely new and fresh approach to archaeology which provoked an awakening interest in aerial photography as a method of determining archaeological sites.

At a cost of 50 shillings, (over a week's wages to a fairly well paid working man) the volume was out of the reach of the majority of the population, who were confined to reading the reviews in national newspapers. One such review noted that 'the views obtained of Prehistoric camps and sites are magnificent, and the book will serve as a handbook of field archaeology for both expert and amateur'.[54] This new and innovative work proved to be popular with academic readers in Britain, and further afield in Europe.

Upon the conclusion of his air sorties from Andover, Keiller presented the RAF Mess with a dozen standard works on archaeology. Following the interest shown there particularly in flint implements, Keiller suggested his friend the Reverend Kendall as an expert in this subject 'to guide their faltering steps',[55] much to Kendall's delight.

Negotiations for the land purchase were concluded on 8th October, when Keiller became owner of most of the Windmill Hill site for a sum of £510.10s.

After a brief spell abroad, and a traditional break at his home in Morven for the shooting season, Keiller returned to London with Veronica to supervise the alteration of their home. Shortly after his marriage Keiller had bought the lease on the adjoining house in Charles Street, No. 3, and set about having the two dwellings converted into one. Initially, an upstairs room was allocated for his and Veronica's combined collection of artefacts, but owing to the unexpected increase in volume with additions from Kendall and other sources, Keiller decided to use the entire ground floor as his own private museum. To this end he added: 'The second floor I will absorb for my library, the third floor our respective bedrooms and bathrooms, the fourth my dear old Brown Study, map room and drawing office, with my secretaries being perilously perched on the roof...'.[56]

The walls of his Brown Study and map room as well as the top of the drawing and map cases, were all covered with an imitation leather. He had stools made with leather seats which were stamped with the name of their designated room, and on removing the padded seat the stools could be used as waste paper bins.[57] All of his

Fig. 13. The Library at 4 Charles Street, London, in 1923   *WA&NHS Library, Devizes*

photo albums were bound in levant, or imitation levant. In later years he was extremely irritated at one point to find that his most recent album had been returned to him bound in a hard grained morocco, and 'a rather unpleasant one at that'. The perpetrator, Wallace Heaton, received a sound reprimand and was extremely apologetic about the misdemeanour.[58]

14
THE TULIPWOOD CAR

IT WAS PROBABLY on his return from Switzerland in January of 1925 that Keiller discovered the 'Tulipwood Car'. The story of its acquisition is as follows...
Somewhere in France Keiller was travelling down a long straight road, probably testing the abilities of his car, when something unheard of happened – another car passed him. He ordered his driver to give chase but the car could not be caught. Following the direction the car had taken, they found it parked outside a hotel. The car, an Hispano Suiza, belonged to a Monsieur Coty, and after some negotiation it passed into the hands of Alexander Keiller.

This story was related by Stuart Piggott, who recalled the car because Keiller once allowed him to drive it on the Avebury – Devizes road, and he attained a speed of 100mph for the first time as driver.[59]

The car itself has an interesting history. Internationally known as the Tulipwood Car, it is thought by some to be the most beautiful car ever made.

Fig. 14. The Tulipwood Car *NMM Library, Beaulieu*

HISPANO-SUIZA[60]

Hispano-Suiza was a Spanish company whose name derives from both its country of origin (Hispano), and that of its principal designer and engineer Marc Birkigt who was Swiss (Suiza). The company enjoyed royal patronage, but the market was poor in Spain compared to the rich potential of northern Europe and so the decision was made to open a factory in Paris.

It was here that the advanced design H6 was first built and introduced to the world. The luxurious nature and appeal of the car attracted a wealthy clientele, and there was a wide variety of lavish custom-built coachwork designs available to be fitted to the H6 chassis. One such owner, Andre Dubonnet of the aperitif dynasty, realized the racing potential of his new car. To prove his theory he entered his four-seater H6 in the Coupe Boillot at Boulogne in 1921, and promptly walked away with the championship.

Spurred on by this victory, the Hispano-Suiza company prepared four cars to compete as a team in the Coupe Boillot the following season. These cars differed from production models in a variety of ways, which included a shortened chassis, engine modifications and light bodywork to reduce the weight of the car. The team won not only at Boulogne, but also at Monza, and further modification ensured undisputed success in 1923. This was the last appearance of the Hispano-Suiza team, but Dubonnet was not deterred and entered one of the 'Boulogne' models, as they had become known, in other races such as the Targa and Coppa Florio in Sicily. Both of these races were held on Sunday 27th April, with the former being four laps of the circuit and the latter five. One drawback with the H6 was its healthy appetite for tyres when racing due to weight, and Dubonnet managed only sixth and fifth place in the respective races against the lighter and more agile Italian competitors. Perhaps for this reason he later sold the car.

The name 'Tulipwood Car' was given due to the magnificent coachwork, made entirely of tulipwood which was copper riveted to the light aluminium body by the same method as would have been found with an aircraft. This similarity was not surprising due to the fact that the body was constructed by Nieuport-Astra, a French aeroplane manufacturer.

Fig. 15. The Hispano-Suiza and MG at Harford Bridge Flats, with Kay Duncan, Susan Palmer and Keiller's driver *Susan Palmer*

The fastest recorded speed of the car was 125mph, which was not surprising with an engine capacity of 7,982cc developing 175bhp. By the time Keiller bought the car it had already been converted for road use. He brought it to England and it was registered 'XX 3883' early in 1925.

Dubonnet had not bothered to fit wings or a windscreen for racing, but a photograph taken at Brooklands in 1925 shows a stylish set of flared front and rear wings which in no way detracted from the sporting image of the car.

Keiller mentions the Hispano-Suiza in a letter to a colleague dated 1932, where he refers to it fondly as 'Hippy'. It would be around this time that the young Stuart Piggott had the opportunity to take the car up to a comfortable 100mph, cutting a swathe through the Wiltshire countryside without really having to push 'Hippy' to her limits.

The car remained in Keiller's ownership for 25 years until discovered in a coach-builder's storehouse in London by Rodney Forestier-Walker in 1950. He contacted Keiller, and was invited to tea at his house. It was then that the car passed from Keiller's ownership, and after many journeys both in Europe and the United States it came finally to rest at the Behring Auto Museum in Danville, California where it can now be appreciated by all who visit.[61]

15
WINDMILL HILL – The Early Years

DURING THE FIRST months of 1925, following his winter break at St Moritz, Keiller enlisted the help of his colleague Crawford to organise an archaeological excavation on his newly purchased land at Windmill Hill. Despite the fact that he owned the land, his proposal caused considerable opposition from the Curator of the Devizes Museum, Maud Cunnington, and members of the Wiltshire Archaeological Society.

The Cunnington family had a long history of involvement with archaeology in Wiltshire. In the early 1800s, William Cunnington (I), with Richard Colt Hoare, directed early excavations at Stonehenge at a time when archaeology was virtually an unknown subject.[62]   In 1865, William Cunnington (III) was involved with further excavations which determined that Avebury was not a cemetery as had been previously supposed, and he was also one of the founders of the Wiltshire Archaeological and Natural History Society.[63]

Maud Cunnington was curator of the Museum at Devizes, headquarters of the Wiltshire Archaeological Society. She and her husband Benjamin, great-grandson of William Cunnington (I), had undertaken many excavations in the Avebury area.

Fig. 16. Maud Cunnington   *WA&NHS Library, Devizes*

They had erected 'Adam', one of two surviving stones from the possible Beckhampton Avenue and Cove, in 1911, and in 1912 another stone in the West Kennet Avenue. In 1930 they had uncovered the location of the Sanctuary on Overton Hill, and directed an excavation of the site which gave us most of the information we know about it today.[64]

In short, Wiltshire was the Cunningtons' domain, and as an unknown outsider Keiller was inadvertently treading on the toes of renowned local archaeologists. Crawford acted as mediator, and it was eventually agreed that excavation could commence on Windmill Hill on the understanding that Harold St George Gray would be the nominal director. Gray had learned his methods under the supervision of General Pitt Rivers, a man who had revolutionised techniques in excavation during the late nineteenth century. Between 1908 and 1914 Gray had spent four seasons excavating at Avebury henge, most notably taking several sections of the southern ditch down to its original level. This was enough to secure him the post of Director for the Windmill Hill excavation, with the approval of both the Cunningtons and Keiller.[65]

Gray's one proviso was that he be permitted to employ William Young as his foreman. Young had embarked upon a career in archaeology after the First World War, working initially with Dr R. C. C. Clay on Iron Age settlements in Wessex before progressing by experience to the position of foreman.[65a]

The first season on Windmill Hill began on April 16th 1925, with the assistance of both Keiller's wife Veronica and her sister Dorothy Liddell. That first morning must have been filled with a nervous trepidation for all concerned. Some archaeological sites hold interest for the visitor purely on the basis of what remains

Fig. 17. Harold St George Gray   *Alexander Keiller Museum, Avebury*

there for them to see; others, no less significant, because of what once was there. Windmill Hill falls into both of these categories, but to anyone who has an eye for beauty it is also the location of the site which takes the breath away. Our ancestors must have looked upon an entirely different landscape when they considered the site for their enclosure, with woodland being predominant where there are now rolling green fields. The site would not have been chosen then so that we would be able to appreciate now the panoramic views, but more importantly so that it could be seen from far away no matter which direction people were travelling from. Bright bands of chalk ditches would have guided each traveller to the site at the appointed gathering times throughout the year. To the party of archaeologists who arrived on Windmill Hill that first Spring morning the prospect of new discoveries awaiting them beneath the turf must surely have been gilded by the beauty of their surroundings.

Fig. 18. The Windmill Hill team, including K eiller, Veronica, Kay Duncan and Young
Alexander Keiller Museum, Avebury

It soon became obvious that professional relationships would be difficult owing to Keiller's desire to introduce new techniques and equipment, set against Gray's rigid school of nineteenth-century method. Keiller wanted to keep all the finds which came to light, but Gray saw no purpose in keeping animal bone and ordered that it should all be re-buried in the shallow ditches.[66]

WINDMILL HILL

Windmill Hill is the largest of all known Neolithic causewayed enclosures in Britain. Three concentric broken rings of ditches enclose a total area of about 21 acres. Following Keiller's excavations in the 1920s, which established the site as a causewayed enclosure, Windmill Hill came to be used as a type site, giving its name to the Windmill Hill Culture. For several decades this was the favoured definition of the early Neolithic period in Southern Britain, although the term is no longer used. There are many theories as to the purpose of Windmill Hill, such as gathering place or ceremonial site, but it was undoubtedly a place of importance to the people who created it, and succeeding generations.

In a letter to archaeologist V. Gordon Childe in 1928, Keiller noted '...Round Windmill Hill is twined, if we can only disentangle it, the entire story of our earliest direct ancestors in these islands, and far wiser will it be when subsequent civilizations are built up upon the basis of our knowledge there, rather than as at present when we are forced to deduce in reverse, if you see what I mean, from later periods. If I could be given now the data which ... I believe that I shall be able to pass to my successor in a quarter of a century's time, what a picture I could now draw of one of the last pre-Bronze Age civilizations in the West of Europe'.

The three concentric ring ditches seem to have been constructed some time around 3500 BC. Worked stone from as far afield as the Lake District, and pottery from Cornwall suggest wide-ranging contact for the people using it. The vast quantities of animal bone point to large numbers of people converging on the site at a given time, possibly for feasting as a part of religious ceremonies.

The excavations uncovered evidence of ritual activity, burials, and suggested the possibility that the site was a settlement before it became an enclosure: a cluster of thirty-two pits on the east side produced a quantity of worked flint, pottery and sarsen, as well as fragments of oolitic limestone from several miles away. A small square enclosure was discovered with further pits, similar in design to mortuary houses found on other neolithic sites, although there is no evidence of this being a mortuary site at Windmill Hill.

One of Keiller's discoveries in 1928 was the skeleton of a domesticated dog intact. *The Times* reported that Keiller had wished to name the skeleton '*Canis familiaris felstedensis*', for it had been discovered upon Derby day shortly after the entire staff excavating on Windmill Hill had gathered together to hear the result of the race. Keiller's idea of naming his find after the Derby winner 'Felstead' was not greeted favourably by antiquarian fellows, and thus the official name given was '*Canis familiaris palustris*'.[67] This skeleton is still an exhibit at the museum in Avebury.

Only two individual human skeletons were discovered complete. One was of a seven month old infant and the other a three year old child. The latter is set

Fig. 19. The ex cavation of 'Charlie ', the skeleton of a y oung child. N ow a permanent exhibit at the Alexander K eiller M useum in A vebur y *Alexander Keiller Museum, Avebury*

into the floor of the museum in Avebury, which has been its resting place since the 1930s. Other human remains were found but these had been scattered about the site amongst animal bone deposits, seemingly without any consideration or ceremony.

The site is particularly notable for its pottery, with over one thousand round-based vessels being represented mainly by sherds. Copious amounts of worked flint continued to surface, and were all collected by Keiller who removed many of the finds to his private museum at Charles Street in London.

Keiller's purchase in 1924 of William Stukeley's[68] original manuscripts and etchings had fuelled his interest in Stone Circles, not only of the recumbent type. At the conclusion of his first season at Windmill Hill, he speculates that the site might once have been '..a monstrous stone circle; that the stones were removed, presumably to Avebury, and that thereupon the area within the ditch surrounding the outer circle of standing stones was utilised as a habitation site, and one or two other ditches added...'.[69]

The excavation lasted for only three weeks that year, and despite the friction between the two men, Gray arranged to return the following season. Owing to the agreement sanctioned by Crawford, Keiller was not permitted to excavate independently until he had proved his worth to both the Cunningtons and the Wiltshire Archaeological Society.

16
A RICH HERITAGE

KEILLER SPENT the summer months of 1925 at Morven with Veronica, continuing his surveys of megalithic monuments in Aberdeenshire and beyond. They made detailed ink drawings of their findings, with measurements and theodolite readings meticulously recorded. One of that year's surveys was on a small tract of land close to the Morven estate – Burn'o'Vat.[70] Here, in a strange rock enclosure called the Vat through which flows a burn, or stream, it is reputed that Rob Roy McGregor hid from Government troops in the 1700s. Perhaps, for Keiller, as he was entitled to wear the McGregor[71] tartan on account of his mother's maiden name Greig, Burn'o'Vat was of special significance as it was associated with his infamous ancestor.

Fig. 20. Old Keig, Aberdeenshire *Author*

Fig. 21. Recumbent stone cir cle at Cothiemuir Wood, A berdeenshir e
Sharon Darrall

In all, during the 1920s, Keiller was able to complete over 200 of these surveys, including notable sites such as Loanhead of Daviot, and Cothiemuir. The only site whose survey he did not complete, once started, was the Grandmother of all recumbent stone circles, Old Keig. When Gordon Childe was excavating there in 1932, Keiller wrote to him explaining that the survey '..having been commenced, had to be abandoned on account of villainous weather conditions'.[72] Anyone who has ever visited the site will know that despite the beauty of her surroundings, Old Keig is a bleak and otherworldly place.

Keiller published two reports (the Interim [1927] and the Final [1928] Reports upon such of the Stone Circles of Aberdeenshire and Kincardineshire as have been Scheduled as Ancient Monuments), the first holding 31 individual reports, and the second 21 reports. The first pamphlet had a favourable review in *Antiquity* in 1928, and had to be reprinted owing to demand.

He was quite brutally honest in the write-ups on these sites, particularly the high number of neglected ones, with such comments as … 'The condition of this circle is quite hopeless' … 'Shocking; one of the worst examples of disregard on record'. It was not all bad news, however, and on sites such as Aquhorthies the report reads … 'This circle is the best preserved ring of megaliths in the whole of Aberdeenshire, better even than that at Tyrebagger.', and of South Ythsie he writes …'It is pleasant to be able to end this report with a statement that the condition of this Stone Circle is extraordinarily good, all things considered.'[72a]

It must not be forgotten that these summer sojourns also most conveniently fitted in with the grouse shooting season commencing on the 'glorious twelfth'. A field note book from a previous summer, when Keiller had been surveying stone circles, is interspersed with details about his grouse shooting, noting the average amount of successful shots, both before and after lunch. - 'Lower Glen Fenzie, August 14th 1922. Average after lunch 1 in 1.48, i.e. 25 birds shot in 37 shots'.[73]

The winter months were spent, as usual, in St Moritz, and in Spring 1926, Keiller, Veronica and Young visited Ireland prior to the new season at Windmill Hill. In a scathing letter of criticism to Gray shortly before the excavations, Keiller wrote saying that some of the pieces of pot Gray had discarded in the 1925 dig, had been retrieved and found to make up two almost perfect round bottom bowls. In consequence,

'…You see, Mr Gray, I have been brought up to certain preliminary rules of archaeological excavation of which three, as I have always been taught, were of paramount importance.

a) No find should be thrown away until it has been washed.

b) No pottery discarded until it has been proved of no instructional value or could be joined to others.

c) Exact position must be noted and preserved in the case of all finds.

PHONE: AVEBURY 22.
TELEGRAMS: LAWES, AVEBURY.

RED LION HOTEL,
AVEBURY,
MARLBOROUGH,
WILTS.

H. LAWES. PROPRIETOR.

MOTOR LANDAULETTE AND BUSES ON HIRE.

Marlborough Station, 7 miles.
Calne Station, 7 miles.
Swindon Old Town Station, 11 miles.
Wootton Bassett Station, 10 miles.

New and extensive alterations.
Parties catered for up to 200.
Dinners and Teas.
Modern Bedrooms and Offices.

Including Net. Health Insurance. Account of Wages, Avebury (Windmill Hill).
May 1926.

Week ending May 8th	£ 0 - 18 - 8
" " " 15th	8 - 15 - 3
" " " 22nd	* 9 - 11 - 3
" " - 29th	8 - 14 - 9
Contract for filling-in	8 - 10 - 0
	£ 36 - 9 - 11

Labour, 1925.

First ½-week	£ 3 - 5 - 4
Second week	7 - 11 - 7
This week	8 - 19 - 3
Contract, filling-in	7 - 10 - 0
	£ 27 - 6 - 2

Fig. 22. Pay of hands, May 1926 compared to 1925 *Alexander Keiller Museum, Avebury*

The first, the less said about the better, since the saws recovered by my wife were from (flint) flakes you had thrown aside...'.[74]

The letter continues in the same vein, questioning Gray's labelling and recording techniques, which Keiller claims made no sense to anyone but Gray himself.

In May 1926 the Windmill Hill team returned to the site. The 'Permanent Staff' filled the guest rooms at the Red Lion, and also on occasions at Perry's Hotel on the opposite side of the road. The rest of the workforce was made up of local labourers.

Relationships were perhaps a little more testy now, following Keiller's less than subtle letter, and with Keiller himself champing at the bit. He was a man who was used to taking charge, yet here he found himself not only answerable to someone else, but also to someone with whom he disagreed on various key issues. His field note book for that season is half filled with Limericks, written in the main by himself, but sometimes in collusion with his wife, all filled with derogatory remarks about Gray.

17
LIMERICKS [75]

THERE WAS an old fool with a tape
Who said "let us try to escape
Surveying new-fangled
All levelled and angled"
So he measured steep slopes with a tape.

There was an old fool with a flake
Who said " 'Tis a grievous mistake
To keep what you've found
– There's lots more in the ground.
We never do down at the Lake."

There was an old fool with a spade
Who said "I will come to your aid.
You choose your direction
And slice off a section
To find out how pottery's made".

There was an old fool with a fork
Who attacked a sheer wall of the chalk,
Shouting -"Widen it, man,
Till it equals the plan:
After all, it's my drawings that talk."

There was an old fool with a shard
Who said, "If I scratch at it hard,
I can do quite a lot
To embellish a pot
And 'a pattern' looks good on the card".

Nineteen-Twenty-Seven was Gray's final year at Windmill Hill. He left on May 26th during the middle of the season, being driven to Swindon railway station in Veronica's Lancia. From that point onwards Keiller became sole director of the excavations. He ordered immediately that the ditch segments previously excavated in 1925 should be re-opened, and the animal bone which Gray had discarded be removed for examination. He announced to Crawford his intention to excavate the entire site apart from a control sample to be left for future generations.[76] A further part of this plan was to publish excavation reports every three years.

One of the unusual sights on Windmill Hill at this time was the Citroën 'Caterpillar' Kegresse which was brought down from Scotland by Keiller specifically for the task of travelling across the vast and uneven terrain which the excavation covered. Early cine film shows the Citroen moving unmanned from one side of the site to the other.[77] During recent work in Avebury a section of the 'Caterpillar' track was discovered in a dried out pond which had been used as a household waste dump by Keiller during the 1930s, although sadly the vehicle was destroyed in a garage fire in 1945.

18
THE 'CATERPILLAR'[78]

THIS UNORTHODOX VEHICLE had been designed by Adolphe Kegresse in 1913. He was then head of the Imperial Garage in Russia, and was asked by the Tzar to solve the problem of driving in snow. The first half-track was developed and run that same year. On returning to France, Kegresse showed the idea to André

Fig. 23. The Citroën Kegresse outside the Red Lion, Avebury
Alexander Keiller Museum, Avebury

Citroën who immediately bought the sole rights. Prototypes proved tremendously effective on snow passes, being able to climb gradients as steep as one in three. In 1922 five of these vehicles crossed the Sahara desert, covering a distance of 2000 miles in 22 days and using an astonishing 200 gallons of fuel each. World-wide coverage of this feat boosted sales, and Keiller, who was always interested in new and innovative products, was one of the first to buy a Kegresse and ship it back to Britain. It was registered as 'SA 6623', 'SA' being the old registration letters for the county of Aberdeenshire.

The Dundee Courier reported that Keiller aimed to experiment with the 'Caterpillar' Kegresse for various purposes such as haulage and agricultural use. He had explained to the reporter how the vehicle was able to take ski attachments on the front wheels and thus could be utilised during the long winter months, where deep snow had occasionally cut off those living in his vicinity at Morven from much needed supplies.[79]

The car had been fitted with a four seater body, and was to be used for practical and recreational purposes in Scotland, varying from fetching the laundry from the village to hauling large rocks. During the shooting season, it carried down no fewer than 250 head of game from the Lodge in one journey, and following this impressive performance it was decided to put the vehicle to the ultimate test. Thus, one cold autumn morning, Keiller, together with his uncles James Greig and John Keiller Greig, set off in the Kegresse to conquer the steep slopes of Morven Hill, an elevation of 2862ft /871m. The higher ground was capped with snow, and in places the gradient was one in three, with terrain alternating between treacherous peat bogs, deep heather and large moss covered boulders.

The journey was not intended as a speed trial, and some game shooting was done along the way. The car made the ascent without any real difficulty, but on reaching the cairn that marked the summit, the occupants found the cold so intense that the vehicle was promptly turned around for an immediate and hurried descent. Following the success of this venture, other climbs in the Cairngorms were accomplished before the Kegresse was transported down to the relatively gentle slopes of the Wiltshire Downs for the Windmill Hill excavations.[80]

Fig. 24. The 'Caterpillar' at Windmill Hill, Avebury, 1927
Alexander Keiller Museum, Avebury

19
ANTIQUITY

FOLLOWING A VISIT to the site in late spring 1926, Crawford wrote to Keiller regarding a plan he had been working on for an archaeological journal. After consulting with colleagues in the printing business, and working out a format for his first issue, Crawford approached Keiller to request a loan of £100 to launch his venture. Keiller agreed readily. Most of the loan money was used sending out leaflets to over 20,000 prospective subscribers from a list compiled by Crawford. Enough positive replies were returned to ensure that the demand was there, and *Antiquity* was born.[81] Its success was phenomenal, and circulation is now world-wide. Twelve months later Crawford repaid Keiller the £100 plus an interest payment of £5. He thanked him for the loan, adding that without Keiller's help ' ... it would have been exceedingly difficult, and certainly very risky, to have made such a venture ...'.[82] In his autobiography *Said and Done*, first published in 1955, Crawford states only that a friend loaned him the money to launch *Antiquity*. This was due to Keiller's own request to remain anonymous.

Curiously, however, Crawford does not mention Keiller in his book when referring to *Wessex from the Air*, or in any other context. Despite the fact that the two men assisted each other in various ventures over the years, it seems that their relationship existed purely on a professional basis and did not extend to personal friendship.

Perhaps due to the premature independence brought about by being educated away from home, and the death of both parents at an early age, Keiller found it difficult to form bonds of friendship. He certainly had an extensive circle of acquaintances, and his exuberant personality seems always to have drawn people to him like a magnet, but throughout his days he was at the heart of it a solitary man. He demanded attention through his work and his actions, but in many instances used his wealth and importance to help others, often without taking the credit himself.

20
STONEHENGE

ONE OF THE TOPICS of discussion when Crawford visited the excavation at Windmill Hill in 1927 was the preservation of other important archaeological sites. This subject, especially Stonehenge, was mulled over further during an arranged luncheon appointment at 'Jules' in London.[83]

During the War, an aerodrome had been erected close to Stonehenge. Huge hangars dwarfed the great sarsens, dominating the landscape and making the site an eyesore. Crawford's friend Sir John Squire, editor and founder of *The London Mercury*, who also attended the luncheon with Crawford, had made a bet with a colleague that he would persuade the authorities to remove the hangars, which were now derelict. The result of that meeting with Keiller was the decision to form a fundraising committee in order to buy the land surrounding Stonehenge.

Stonehenge itself had been bought and presented to the nation by Sir Laurence Chubb, and saving accidents with low flying aircraft was safe from further harm. Seeing the reasoning behind the appeal, the Ancient Monuments Department of the Office of Works lent their full co-operation to the formation of a Committee. Crawford launched the appeal on August 8th, stating that the sum of £32,000 would be required for the land purchase. The sum was soon raised, and the land was presented to the National Trust, who rapidly demolished the unsightly hangars.

Keiller's interest in Stonehenge did not end here however, and before the appeal had reached its target he wrote to the Office of Works with regards to the housing of finds from the Stonehenge excavations. He offered to buy all finds, the monies being donated towards the appeal, and also build an 'out of sight' museum nearby which would have study facilities and employ a curator. He came up with two designs for museum buildings which were presented to the Office of Works. The first he deemed a 'possible but not wholly appropriate'[84] design, whilst the second was 'Utopian', and simply produced as an 'experimental essay in idealism'. He also expressed concern over security on the site following an attempt by students to lever a lintel off one of the trilithons. Pointing out that although an appointed night watchman was essential, he would need to be armed with a sufficiently savage dog in order to be a deterrent to future vandals, as the current 'plump spaniel' was ill suited to the task.[85]

Fig. 25. One of Keiller's own Stonehenge Museum plans (© *Giles Currie*)

Keiller's proposals for a museum were not greeted enthusiastically. The Cunningtons wrote to him personally, saying that after all that trouble to get rid of previous buildings near Stonehenge, surely it was not a good idea to build a new one. Even Crawford was of the opinion that the Stonehenge finds should remain in Salisbury.[86]

Keiller wrote a defiant letter to the Office of Works, criticising the Cunningtons' interference in his scheme, and blamed them for 'the agitation aroused, themselves inspired by some form of museum curator's parochial jealousy'. He added that if the Cunningtons 'could possibly be persuaded to regard archaeology as a science and not merely as a personally directed local manifestation emanating primarily and finally from Devizes, not only would the said science of archaeology, but the general advantage of Wiltshire as a County be considerably advanced'.[87] His outburst provoked no response.

Three years later, Keiller finally bowed to the storm of opposition to his proposals and his offer to build a museum was withdrawn.

21
CONFRONTATIONS

TOWARDS THE CLOSE of 1927 Keiller was elected a Fellow of the Society of Antiquaries, and the following year a Fellow of the Geological Society. Of the latter he was particularly proud, and in a letter to Norrington at the Clarendon Press regarding the title page of the Windmill Hill Reports, which were being prepared, he expressed a preference to FGS above all other initials after his name.

Beginning on March 27th 1928 and concluding on April 28th, a series of letters between Keiller and Gray was sparked by a comment made by Gray in a letter to Young (now Keiller's foreman on the Windmill Hill excavations). Gray's letter had included the phrase '..I do not think Mr Keiller ought to make arrangements so late, and to 'chip' in when others are waiting to make definite fixtures..',[88] that pertained to the commencement date of another excavation on which Young was to be present. We must assume that when Young passed on this *he would .* information to Keiller, he could not have known the remark would cause such offence to Keiller, and awaken the dormant temper that simmered beneath a cool exterior.

There was a barrage of angry correspondence on Keiller's part, demanding an apology, whilst an apparently confused Gray failed to understand – or chose not to recognise – the reason for Keiller's personal indignation. Gray eventually withdrew the remarks he had made in Young's letter, an admission which Keiller accepted in the same spirit as it was offered, adding that 'regarding the matter analytically it was a silly muddle all round'.[89] Unfortunately, in the same way as a judge requesting that the jury disregard certain evidence in a trial, what had been said could not be unsaid, and the damage was done. On the surface Keiller seemed happy to let the matter go, but his pride had taken a blow from what he saw as an insult, and he would not easily forget the source of such an apparent slur on his character.

By May things had settled down to an uneasy truce, although Keiller wrote to Gray discussing their conflicting methods of draughtsmanship, having seen some of the work Gray had prepared for the Windmill Hill reports. He referred '..not to results but to the more technical methods employed. It all boils down to this: you learned your draughtsmanship in one school and I learned mine in quite a different one, to wit an engineering factory. In other words, I am a machine draughtsman at heart and, since machine draughtsmen are notoriously pigheaded, stubborn and conservative folk as regards to their job, I am likely to remain so..'.[90]

In late April 1928, the Reverend Kendall died. Since first meeting Kendall, and throughout the course of the Windmill Hill excavations, Keiller and Veronica had spent time with the Kendalls, and in turn Kendall had given them for their collection various flints he had gathered over many years in the Avebury area. Often during the hunting season at Morven, Kendall would be the recipient of a brace of grouse sent down by Keiller. In July 1926, Keiller wrote to him saying, ' ... I in my turn have broken down and have been through a rather bad time. The cause of my collapse was sunstroke and it has left me very weak. It may amuse you to know, however, that during the most frenzied periods of my delirium I kept on stammering "you can find them in every furrow" - doubtless even under these circumstances I was mentally flinting'.[91]   A month after Kendall's death, following a valuation by Dr R. C. C. Clay, Keiller paid £100 to his widow for the remainder of Kendall's flint collection, which was removed to the Charles Street house in London.[92]

22
TAKING THE HELM, 1928-29

NINETEEN-TWENTY-EIGHT was Keiller's first season in sole charge at Windmill Hill. He had begun to gather a dedicated team together, including his wife Veronica, his sister-in-law Dorothy Liddell, and Miss Kay Duncan as supervisors, Young as foreman, and other key employees in charge of the workmen. This team was to remain with him until the conclusion of the Windmill Hill excavations.

Sir Charles Peers, Chief Inspector of Ancient Monuments and Historic Buildings with the Office of Works, wrote to Keiller telling him how much his work was appreciated, saying, ' ... It follows on, but far surpasses, the pioneer work of Pitt Rivers, on that crucial period in the story of our county, the later prehistoric era ... '. He suggested that Keiller set up a training school, arguing why should students have to go as far as Egypt when 'Wiltshire was every bit as important'. Keiller replied that he was flattered by the suggestion, but at the present such a venture would get in the way of his work.

Fig. 26. Keiller on site at Windmill Hill, Avebury   *Alexander Keiller Museum, Avebury*

In truth, there was not one archaeologist on Keiller's team who did not benefit from their time spent with him, not only studying the Neolithic but also taking with them his precise planning and recording methods.[93]

Following post-excavation work carried out in London, Keiller returned to his family estate in Scotland for the shooting season. He took Veronica with him, as well as Young, and under the auspices of the 'Windmill Hill Permanent Excavation Staff', they excavated a cairn ring of approximately 37ft in diameter near the Morven Burn. Ring cairns were sometimes built in the centre of recumbent stone circles and cremated bone or pottery often found within.

Only the interior of the cairn was exposed, and a trial section was taken into the wall to establish the method of construction. Excavation showed that the inner 'ditch' was filled with boulders, when no other boulders were present in the vicinity, suggesting that these boulders had been carried there for some special purpose. No charcoal deposits were found, dismissing the use of this particular cairn for a cremated burial. The unpublished excavation report, which rests with the RCAHMS in Edinburgh, concluded that ' there can be no reasonable doubt that this Cairn ring at any rate served a sepulchral purpose, and it is natural to assume that ... the others which lie adjacent to it in this area were built with the same object'.[94]

During the Autumn he was suddenly taken ill and had to spend some time in a Nursing Home in Aberdeen. He went abroad to convalesce following a further relapse in London, but on his return in late November he had another serious attack of illness during the night, the nature of which is not known. Despite his ill health he was still able to travel to St Moritz over Christmas. Before leaving, he replied to a letter from Gordon Childe, who was about to visit Russia, offering '... fur hats and other articles which I myself last wore in Riga and elsewhere - particularly elsewhere - not so very long ago ...'.[95]

In March of 1929, Keiller was back on the Windmill Hill reports, and wrote to Gray regarding the requested return of some documents, The tone of his letter once again disrupting the fragile pretence of courtesy that the two men displayed publicly. Keiller concluded 'Consequently I must request you let me have these maps and plans by Friday next, March 22nd... Should the whole of the maps and plans of Windmill Hill drawn out by yourself not be in my hands by that date I shall take further steps in the matter immediately in order to obtain their recovery...'[96] The documents were returned and the relationship settled into a cautious truce once more.

The nature of Keiller's illness the previous Autumn is not known, but it continued to trouble him well into 1929. The commencement of the season at Windmill Hill, due May 6th was postponed for three days owing to his ill health. He was well enough to visit the opera in London on the sixth although afterwards at supper in a fashionable restaurant he collapsed. The following day his wife Veronica left for Avebury to prepare for the excavation. Kay Duncan travelled with him from London to Avebury in the Bugatti, and excavations commenced on the ninth.

In late May a young archaeologist named Stuart Piggott wrote to Keiller asking if he might visit the excavations at the allotted time set aside for visitors, being a Saturday afternoon. Keiller's reply was enthusiastic, demonstrating his dry sense of humour and an obvious improvement in health and spirits. He declared that Piggott was '... the only man during the whole of this season who had even suggested visiting the site on visitors day and for this we are all of us much indebted to you'.[97]

In general Keiller was not enthusiastic about visitors, and in earlier seasons had referred to their '... unedifying behaviour, in that they were in the habit of jumping into the cuttings and stamping about in them, and even grubbling about with trowels and forks... '.[98] The latter part of this remark related to a recent visit by Arthur D Passmore, a fellow archaeologist for whom in later years Keiller developed a great deal of respect as a field archaeologist.

Fig. 27. Lunch time off site, Windmill Hill excavations
Alexander Keiller Museum, Avebury

53

In 1928, Piggott, under the directorship of E C Curwen, had been working on 'The Trundle', a hillfort in West Sussex within which had been discovered a ditched enclosure of Neolithic date, similar to Windmill Hill. The visit to Keiller's excavation in 1929 inspired Piggott, on his return to 'The Trundle' the following year, to lay out 'a formal rectilinear cutting in the Windmill Hill manner', where previously technique had been 'rather primitive, with the turf hacked off the appropriate area of excavation'.[99]

Reginald Smith of the British Museum visited The Trundle excavation in 1930, wearing a dark suit, bowler hat and pince-nez glasses, and on seeing Piggott's work declared it 'very marmaladish'.[100] This remark perhaps reflected the professional attitude towards amateur archaeologists with no formal education in the subject, or even hinted at a more deep-seated contempt for those amateur archaeologists whose money enabled them to take a more inquisitive approach, asking questions and searching more diligently for answers and new methods instead of taking the old school presumption that there was nothing more to be learned.

On July 9th 1929, the final day of the Windmill Hill excavation, Keiller had an horrific car accident some miles from Avebury, whilst travelling with Miss Duncan in his Targa Florio Bugatti. He wrote to Gray later that year '... The actual site of the crash you must know well. It is the Railway Bridge on the hill climbing into Savernake out of Marlborough on the main Bath Road . We were climbing this hill at a reasonable speed, but not by any manner of means, I consider, an excessive one, viz. some 84 miles an hour, when my back axle broke and, the car turning round and rising into the air, we hurtled ourselves on to the angular portion of the Bridge. It was fortunate that we hit the angle, since otherwise, considering the speed at which we were travelling, we must have burst through the brick-work and fallen another forty feet on to the Railway line below. It is of course miraculous that either of us lived through the experience.'[101]

In fact, both Keiller and Miss Duncan broke a shoulder-blade and sustained some muscular damage. Keiller also ruptured some internal organs on the impact with the steering wheel, and suffered from severe haemorrhage for quite some time. Various other complications set in, and he was consequently laid up for several months.

23
BUGATTI

KEILLER'S ASSOCIATION with Bugatti's began in 1926. On the first of March that year he told Crawford ' The Grand Prix Bugatti turns out to be a very great vehicle. This morning on about half throttle I attained my ambition to touch

Fig. 28. Keiller with his Type 35 Bugatti, 1926 *Bugatti Trust*

100mph on a British road. She is reputed to be capable of 124, and, having driven her, I can well believe it.'[102]

In Hugh Conway's book *Grand Prix Bugatti*[103] there is a signed photo of Keiller dated 1926, wearing his kilt and standing beside a Bugatti Type 35 registered YM 9558. This car was an 8-cylinder 2-litre model. The car was sold to Aubrey Esson-Scott circa 1930 and was raced at Brooklands in May 1933, taking fastest lap at 109.27mph.

In May of 1927, records indicate that a Bugatti Type 35TC, chassis number 4849, reg. NAE 194, was delivered to Keiller in London.[104]   The initials 'TC' indicate that it was the most potent version of that racing car then available. The 'T' stands for Targa Florio and indicates a 2.3 litre engine, whilst 'C' is for 'compressore' or supercharged. The 'NAE' registration suggests that the car was re-registered at some point, signifying either that it had a new chassis, or as a means of qualifying for reduced road tax.

The Type 35TC models corresponded to the Type 35B. It is known that Keiller owned one of these Type 35Bs, and although he never raced it, successive owners did. In the late 1930s it was sold to racing driver and motorcycle racer Charles Mortimer who bought it for £150.[105]

Against the walls of his garage at Morven in Scotland, the chassis of crashed vehicles hung like hunters' trophies. To Keiller, the twisted metal was an object of pride, for to him it was a tribute to the fact that he had escaped the accident alive. To his disapproving uncle and erstwhile guardian, it was a sign of his nephew's apparent disregard for speed and danger, and the value of his own life. The chassis are long since gone, but the mechanic's pit, and the hoists for pulling out the engines, still remain in what is now a maintenance building for the current owners of the estate.

At Morven, and the nearby town of Ballater, Keiller's sports cars were a source of immense interest in an area where there were few such extravagant motor vehicles. Often, when he drove down through the town, people would come out of their houses and shops to watch him go by, the roar of the engine ricocheting off the buildings as he passed. A cousin of his remembers, at a very early age, being allowed to ride from the Morven Lodge, used then only as a base for shooting forays, down the hillside to the house with Keiller in one of his Bugattis. Travelling at what must have seemed a high speed, bumping over the rough terrain, she recalls he lost his

Fig. 29. Keiller with driver, in Type 35 Bugatti   *Winifrid Jarman, Wroughton*

Tam-o-shanter hat (for he had been shooting in his kilt as was customary), and waved it off as though it didn't matter. The small child was shocked by his attitude, but the loss of a hat was nothing compared to the thrill of the ride.[106]

In 1928 Keiller was asked to take his racing staff, complete with Bugattis, to the Targa Florio race in Italy. Unfortunately the race fixture clashed with the Windmill Hill excavation and Keiller had to decline.[107]

Although Keiller enjoyed road racing, and had a long association with Brooklands, he had never participated in any races, preferring to put together teams to race his cars on the circuit. Who knows whether the excavation was merely an excuse for not racing, or more likely that he was torn between the prospect of his second season as sole director at Windmill Hill, and the one chance for racing glory at the Targa Florio?

24
SUSPICIONS

NINETEEN-TWENTY-NINE saw the conclusion of Keiller's excavations on Windmill Hill, and the end of this period also signified the beginning of problems between Keiller and his wife Veronica. She reflected later that as his interest in archaeology grew, so his affection for her dwindled.

He made a new circle of friends in London, from which Veronica was excluded, and most certainly she was never introduced to any of them. She questioned this on more than one occasion, but received no satisfactory reply from her ill-humoured husband. Having lived with his moods for so long, she knew better than to antagonise him, and let the matter drop.

The house at Charles Street had been altered, so that the ground floor became the museum, the first floor the Map Room, Study, Library, with living rooms taking up only the bare minimum of space. Staff did not live on the premises, but came in daily to work, and owing to the museum there was no longer a proper kitchen. Veronica found it almost impossible to have any semblance of a normal home life. She had to eat all of her meals out except breakfast, and often on her own, as Keiller's busy work schedule and new friends meant that she did not see him a great deal. Already she had her suspicions of his infidelity, but because of her feelings for him, which had not faltered, she chose to ignore what might be happening in the hope that everything would settle down in the future. This was not to be, for later in the year Keiller asked her for a divorce, quite blatantly stating his adultery as the reason. Veronica refused.[108]

25
MISSED OPPORTUNITIES

FOLLOWING A RATHER TRAUMATIC year, both physically and emotionally, it took Keiller some time to get back to matters archaeological, but he began with the Windmill Hill Reports in 1930. By May he had the first draft of the 1928 report together, but was hindered by various delays which were out of his control with regard to maps and plans not in his possession. A month later he told Hogarth at the Clarendon Press, 'I am by degrees building up that most unpleasant reputation that an archaeologist can have, to wit, failure to publish the results of his work in the field'.[109]   By October, he had entered into a legal agreement with the Clarendon Press for the publication of the reports, in which he was required to pay a sum of £200 for initial costs, the balance to be paid by himself on completion.

Ten months later, after endless time-consuming adjustments, Keiller declared to Norrington that there was such an infinite quantity of alterations which needed to be made to the draft copy that publication must be delayed somewhat. He suggested that the format be changed to the size of *Wessex from the Air*, and that the work be produced in two volumes appearing synchronously, ' ... the first volume to comprise 1925 -1928, thus giving the first lamentable year of Gray's directorship, the second year of endeavour to curb his inefficiency, the third year which comprised his exposure and dismissal, and the fourth year which was the first of unified and independent control ...'. The second volume was to contain 'nothing but the superb 1929 Report, which is as complete as a report from Windmill Hill could ever be...'.[110]

Finally Keiller wrote to say that his assistant Miss James[111] had found so many alterations that needed doing it would be impossible for the reports to be published in the foreseeable future. With a long delay inevitable, Keiller had broken the agreement with the Clarendon Press. He admitted to Norrington that the loss (financial) would be considerable to him, but felt, '... Better that, than ... one should continue one's work for the rest of one's life dissatisfied with one of one's chief productions'.[112]

Despite his grand intentions, the Windmill Hill reports were not published until after his death when his widow commissioned Isobel Smith, who had recently completed her doctoral thesis on Neolithic pottery, to undertake the task.

In August 1930 Keiller and Kay Duncan visited the excavation at Hembury Fort in Devon conducted by his sister-in-law Dorothy Liddell, on their way to see Miss Duncan's father at Honiton. William Young, the Windmill Hill foreman, was assisting Miss Liddell with the excavations, and was proud that ' ...Mr K was very impressed ... If we had not followed the Windmill Hill methods I really don't know where we should have been'.[113]   Keiller suggested to him that he began to keep diaries of his archaeological work, for which Keiller would pay him to write up in the winter months when he could not find an income from any other source. Young was to write the following winter, 'I cannot find words to express how grateful I am to him ... Were it not for his help in the past I should long ago have been obliged to throw up archaeology altogether'.[114]   The diaries, some 30 volumes, are now in the Wiltshire Archaeological Society Library at Devizes in Wiltshire.

Following the horrific accident in the Bugatti, Keiller began to look closer to home for a sports car, and chose the new British MG Midget. A reference to his new car in September 1930 states '... The MG landed us up here magnificently [at Morven], in fact Miss Duncan and I had the best run that I have ever had from London to Ballater in my life, or at least if not the fastest, certainly the most enjoyable...We, with my friends the Moores,[115] enjoyed every minute of the two days that we spent on the road, and I became even more enthusiastic about the MG than I was before I started; an opinion which its performance under drastic Aberdeenshire conditions up here has done nothing to mitigate ... As I said to my mechanic when I came in from a solitary run the other night "I never wish a better car than this, and indeed I doubt very much whether I would wish for any other..."[116] Stuart Piggott recalls in one instance driving to Norwich for a meeting of the Prehistoric Society of East Anglia 'rather fast, in Keiller's MG Midget'.[117] This car has not been traced thus far, although a resident at Avebury recalls the fire in the Manor garage in January 1945 which destroyed some of Keiller's cars. Perhaps the MG was amongst them.

26
SKIING MATTERS

IN 1931 KEILLER was elected President of the Ski Club of Great Britain (S.C.G.B.). This accolade demonstrated the depth of his contribution to the Ski Club over many years. Every December and January saw him in St Moritz where he first learned to ski, though as early as 1912 his reputation for speed and courage on the slopes was well established.

He had first put on skis at the impressionable age of fifteen, and had swiftly begun to master the necessary skills. Although his most frequent winter haunt was Switzerland, he also took to the ski runs in Norway and the mountains of Scotland. Of Morven, he said that he had ski'd her steep sides in Winter, and they had surpassed anything he'd had in Canada, and compared not unfavourably with Switzerland or Central Europe.[118]

Fig. 30. The 'Keillerschanze' ski jump in Badrutt Park, Switzerland   *Bibliothek St Moritz*

Surrounded by the local guides and professional instructors of the 'Ski Club Alpina' from the very early days, he received rigorous training both in technique and endurance. He first competed in a British event in 1913, and won the S.C.G.B. cup for the longest jump – 84ft 6in /25.8m – improving on that in the same competition the following season with a jump of 88ft 6in /27m, and even longer jumps elsewhere.[119]

The War from 1914-1918 put a temporary halt to this winter pastime, what with commitments at home and abroad during military service. However, during the year when Keiller was not on active service after being invalided out of the R.N.A.S., he managed to get out to St Moritz in 1917 for five days and indulge in his sport.

In the 1920s he developed his interest in another particular form of skiing, namely langlauf [crosscountry], but he was still an active ski jumper, and was honoured in the Engadine for jumping a distance of 30 metres in Davos. Near St Moritz he built the Innschanze, a practice jump, and then in the Badrutt Park, another jump was redesigned and built with his help. The Swiss officially named it the Keillerschanze to perpetuate the memory of the benefactor who had done so much to help them.[120]

As early as 1924 he was heavily involved with the official side of the sport. Wallace Heaton,[121] a friend and colleague who had written to him for advice on equipment, and who was to be in St Moritz at the same time as Keiller, was told, '... I personally shall not be very far away, although this year I am afraid that all my time is going to be taken up with secretaryships and other official work as I seem to be the committee or club representative of every organization which at present exists in the skiing world.'[122]

An article in the 1926 S.C.G.B. *Ski Notes and Queries* praises Keiller's tireless administrative work, stating that he spent the major part of his winter holidays carrying out duties as the Technical Committee Representative in Switzerland, as well as his responsibilities as a member of no less than four other ski clubs.

Fig. 31. Keiller in St Moritz, 1926, from 'Prominent Ski Runners', S.C.G.B. *Ski Club of Great Britain*

In 1927 the Langlauf Club was formed as an affiliate of the S.C.G.B., and from 1928-31 Keiller was Editor of both the British Langlauf Club and the British Ski Jump Club publications. His wife Veronica was Honorary Secretary of the Langlauf Club in 1930, and also made occasional contributions to the S.C.G.B. Yearbook. 1928 saw him captaining the winning St Moritz jumping team for the Engadine Challenge Cup even though he had jolted his spine on the journey out from England. He was elected President of the British Ski Jump Club in 1930, with Veronica as Honorary Secretary.

The year of his S.C.G.B. Presidency was a full one, and early in December of 1931 he went to Canada with the Oxford and Cambridge University teams. A photograph in the 1932 Ski Club Yearbook shows him receiving an Honorary Member's badge for the 'Seigniory Club of Lucerne-in-Quebec'. The visit was a complete success, with the British University teams beating their Canadian opponents.

Keiller described his position there as 'trainer, manager, doctor, pedicurist and everything else as well' to twenty of the nicest fellows he had ever met, adding that they all knew each other by Christian names, and indeed 'just about as well as was possible'.[123]   Their team spirit impressed the Canadians, which particularly pleased Keiller who commented that 'Varsity teams did not usually shine in such aspects'.

A whimsical remark made by the Norwegian President of the Ski Club of Montreal struck a note with Keiller. Looking at him shrewdly Johannsen had said 'You must get one great kick from being with those young fellows', to which Keiller replied that this was extraordinarily true, and seldom had he enjoyed himself more.[124]

In March following their return to England, Keiller attended the Oxford University Ski Club Dinner, where '..sixteen of us consumed a hundred and fifty cocktails before the meal began. I clearly recollect doing my share up to this point, after which point I do not very clearly recollect anything ...'.[125]

In December of 1932 Keiller returned once more to St Moritz to judge the skiing, and as trainer and manager of the British team. He had an accident whilst ski jumping which badly damaged his shoulder, and for months afterwards this injury seems to have been a severe handicap. There is little mention of skiing after, so perhaps the injury prevented him in later years from pursuing his sport, although he still visited St Moritz as late as 1947 when he travelled there with his fourth wife. Piggott recalls being at Keiller's house in Charles Street, when upon seeing the file entitled 'Skiing Matters' lying on his secretary's desk, Keiller remarked, 'Does it?'.[126]

His obituary in the Ski Club Yearbook states that 'credit for the rising British interest in Langlauf and Jumping [during the Twenties and Thirties] must in very large measure go to him, and that there was no doubt that in those early years his unbounded enthusiasm and his remarkable personal knowledge of technique brought about British participation in these branches of skiing. The Swiss loved him, and many found their way, in the inter-war years, either to his beautiful Scottish home at Ballater or to his house in Charles Street, where the Alpina shield hung over his door. Certainly for him skiing was far more than a winter pastime for the rich. He pursued it as a sport with dedication, and would be remembered for the excellent standards he set for others to follow.'[127]

27
RECOGNITION

APRIL 1932 saw one of the Windmill Hill Permanent Staff, Kathleen (Kay) Duncan, leave the confines of the Keillers' employ for pastures new. Unlike many of his female acquaintances, where Kay Duncan was concerned Keiller harboured honourable intentions. He had wished to marry her, but it is apparent Veronica refused a divorce unless Kay was named. Kay's father was a minister, and her brothers were convinced that the shame of his daughter being branded an adulterer in a divorce hearing would be too much for him. Perhaps, with Veronica's continuing refusal to divorce on any other grounds, Kay decided to make a fresh start somewhere with fewer reminders of her doomed romance. Through Norrington, Keiller managed to secure for her a post at the Clarendon Press in Oxford. For a brief time, things went well. Keiller himself spent a considerable amount of time in Oxford both on archaeological matters and on a social level. Shortly after the move he took a party, including Miss Duncan, the Norringtons, and his friends the Moores, to see a D'Oyly Carte production of 'The Mikado'. In the letter of invitation to Norrington, he reminisced that his first ever visit to a theatre – the Savoy – had been in 1895 with his mother to see 'The Mikado'.

Kay Duncan's position in Oxford was not to last long, and owing to a misunderstanding over her job description she was forced to give up her post. An outraged Keiller wrote a lengthy complaint to the company in her defence, but it was too late. She left Oxford, having no work there, and in doing so ended a long chapter in her own life and Keiller's.[128]

In 1932, Keiller helped to organise the First International Congress on Prehistoric and Protohistoric Sciences. On August 4th he lectured to the Congress on the Excavations at Windmill Hill. The lecture was reported upon twice in *The Times* newspaper, who said that his discoveries had made one of the most important of all contributions to British Prehistory. The excavations, they went on, had been done with the utmost exactitude and efficiency, and without sparing expense.[129]

This was Keiller's first public speech, and Prof V Gordon Childe concluded that to persuade Keiller to speak publicly about his excavation work had surely been one of the Congress's chief achievements, and the review noted, 'Everyone was delighted by his [Keiller's] modest demeanour, for he had the slightly haunted look of a Rugger Blue facing his degree examiners and uncertain of the result.'[130]

Keiller's speech was heard by several 'up and coming' archaeologists who recall it well, one of these being a young Leslie Grinsell.[131] Following the lecture in the morning, which described all manner of finds from flints to the complete skeletons discovered including *Canis familiaris palustris* Keiller opened his private museum at 4 Charles Street to members of the Congress. It was noted that ...'The four magnificent skeletons and the thousands of flints and pieces of pottery were exhibited beautifully ...'. *The Times* concluded by saying that ' it was not a little odd that the discovery of a domesticated neolithic dog should have been made possible through the consumption of a very well known domestic product, as Keiller was a member of the family of Dundee preserve manufacturers, and his excavations could not have been made without much wealth.'[132]

The week following his successful debut Keiller travelled up to his Scottish home in Morven for the shooting season, accompanied by his wife and her sister Dorothy. Their return was somewhat delayed when Dorothy Liddell was taken seriously ill and had to convalesce in an Aberdeen nursing home.

28
BARROWS AND WHEELER

FOLLOWING THEIR INITIAL MEETING at Windmill Hill in Avebury during the late twenties, Stuart Piggott was invited by Keiller to study the finds from the site which were housed in the private museum at Charles Street. At the time Piggott was preparing a Paper entitled 'The Neolithic Pottery of the British Isles', which was published shortly afterwards in the *Archaeological Journal.*

Quite often during this period, Keiller used to suggest that they went out to lunch at around 12.30 – usually at either the Berkeley, Grosvenor or Mayfair Hotels. Keiller was prone to bouts of stomach upset, perhaps as a result of his injuries in the Bugatti accident, and always carried some toilet paper in his inside breast pocket. On one occasion the waiter came to the table with the bill, and Keiller, who was in conversation with Piggott at the time, paid the waiter with the toilet paper. When he realised what had happened he laughed so loudly, that Piggott recalled he 'rendered the whole dining room silent!'.[133]

With the opening of the Charles Street museum for students studying the Neolithic period, it became apparent that modern excavation of other types of Neolithic sites in Wessex was a pressing need, in order to add more pieces to the

Fig. 32. W.E.V. Young, 1933 *WA&NHS Library, Devizes*

jigsaw puzzle. In March 1933, Piggott wrote to Keiller asking if it were possible to borrow some of the excavation equipment which he had purchased for the Windmill Hill digs to use for the excavation of a long barrow at Thickthorn Down in Dorset. Piggott was planning the dig in conjunction with Charles Drew, Curator of Dorchester County Museum, and was trying to keep down expenses as much as possible. On a note of good humour he added ' ... We have managed to secure Young, who will be able to keep an eye on me when I try to falsify evidence, measure up with an umbrella or throw away pot sherds.'[134] This was a veiled reference to the Cunningtons, which no doubt must have delighted Keiller.

Keiller replied favourably, and also offered his assistance for surveying, a task he thoroughly enjoyed. He was still suffering with the ski jumping injury from the previous season, and the prospect of being 'back in the field' again pleased him immensely.[135]

65

Fig. 33. Thickthorn Down excavations, 1933   *Alexander Keiller Museum, Avebury*

The excavation proceeded in June, with Young and Miss James assisting. Young was delighted to find that that barrow was one visited by Keiller after observing it from the air on July 14 1924.[136] Leslie Grinsell recalled visiting the site, and being witness to Keiller's flaming temper which he used on the villagers 'with little or no provocation.'[137]

The excavation must have had special significance for Keiller, as a plan of the barrow held pride of place on the wall of his map room for many years thereafter.

It was during the course of this excavation that he persuaded Piggott to become one of his 'staff', describing him as '... with the possible exception of Christopher Hawkes of the B.M. [British Museum], unquestionably the archaeologist of most promise among the younger generation'.[138] This came about because Piggott had taken all of his annual leave from his post at the Welsh Ancient Monuments Commission in order to work at Thickthorn Down. At the point where his superior, Hemp, visited the site it was quite obvious that the dig would take longer than anticipated, and Piggott begged for an extension of leave. It was refused abruptly. When Keiller learned of the outcome he was furious, and in turn offered Piggott private employment for a higher salary. Despite the fact that the offer was tempting, and Piggott was not happy in his post with the Civil Service, he hesitated in accepting until Crawford assured him that Keiller was 'erratic, and at times infuriating, but a genuine enthusiast, and really loves archaeology'.[139]

In the autumn, Keiller was employed as surveyor to the famous Maiden Castle Excavation under the directorship of Mortimer Wheeler. He considered that Wheeler may have professed an admiration tinctured with affection for himself and his work, but 'on occasion he gave every indication of resenting both'.[140]   He admitted that Wheeler had done some very good work, but he was not fond of the man personally and deprecated certain of his characteristics as well as some of his methods. At a meeting on the site, Keiller took exception to an outburst from Wheeler against him, and consequently resigned from his position as surveyor. Wheeler apologised the following day, but despite the personal rift being 'rivetted up',[140a] Keiller pointed out that in view of Wheeler's attitude he could not foresee the probability of co-operation in the future.

The basis for this disagreement may well have been a degree of professional jealousy. At the time Wheeler was a renowned archaeologist,[141] whereas Keiller, who strove to be recognised and accepted, was still considered by some as an employer of archaeologists. In 1936, Piggott was blackballed (voted against in a membership selection ballot) by the Society of Antiquaries, something which he later learned was due to the unpopularity of his sponsor Keiller, but he was elected the following year. This seems to have been an attitude prevalent South of the Border, as there were no such obstacles for V. Gordon Childe when he and Veronica were put forward by Keiller for the Society of Antiquaries in Scotland in 1927.

In fieldwork, the quality of Keiller's work, the scientific techniques he applied and his methodical approach were meticulous. The image of Victorian gentleman archaeologist was banished to the annals of equally antiquated museum archives. It was replaced with the picture of a dedicated master of his chosen vocation, rather than an eager novice. In 1937 he was to write '..Archaeological excavation can, and indeed must partake of the nature of an exact science. The excavator is the recorder of demonstrable fact; his statements must partake of an accuracy which results in their being unalterable. The technique of the methods which he employs, no less than the instruments which he utilises, must of necessity be scientific in the strictest sense of the term, even as the attitude of mind which he brings to bear upon his task must also in its lack of bias, as well as in its subsequent restraint, be in its essence scientific...'[141a] He was able to hone his skills on the excavations which he funded and undertook at Avebury, work which has benefitted anyone who has visited the site since.

His downfall was the writing of reports. He was so caught up in the technicalities of analysis and description, that there was never an end result to suit his perfectionist nature. He loved the challenge of planning, the excitement of discovery, and the obsessive detail of recording, but in essence he was happier out in the field than producing reports in an office. The Windmill Hill report (together with that on his later work in Avebury) was not finally published until 1965, having been commissioned by his widow after his death.

In the academic world, where funding was minimal, most excavations were small scale and undertaken with limited financial assistance. In contrast Keiller, with his vast inheritance, was able to excavate on a much larger scale. There is no doubt that his contribution to the study of causewayed enclosures was seminal, and that the Windmill Hill excavations uncovered a whole new area in British Neolithic history, but this very fact caused resentment amongst his contemporaries who may, if financed on an equivalent scale, have made equally significant discoveries. One possible reason why Wheeler, for example, is more of a remembered name than Keiller is because he had a clear idea of why he was digging, looking for an answer to a particular problem and pursuing it ruthlessly, whereas Keiller allowed his technical obsession to dominate.

Shame, you let yourself down

29
HARSH WORDS

ON LEAVING MAIDEN CASTLE in the autumn of 1933, Keiller returned to London, and from there travelled to Scotland with Veronica for a spot of grouse shooting. By this time, having seen little of her husband over the previous year, and been shown no signs of his affection, Veronica was at the end of her tether. Whilst Keiller was on a brief trip to London, she poured out her feelings to him in a letter. It was her only option, for she found it impossible to talk to him without him either losing his temper or turning the discussion in other directions.

When Keiller returned to Morven, Veronica gave him the letter. At first, he was very upset, and avoided her for a few days, but when they did finally talk, he would not discuss the contents of the letter. Finally admitting defeat, Veronica returned to their house at Charles Street in London, packed all of her belongings and moved to Sherfield Manor in Hampshire, leaving a note to say she was visiting her mother and sister.

Three weeks later she telephoned Keiller, who had returned to London, and told him plainly that she had left for good, and that she had not told him of this intention previously because she feared his reaction. He made no comment on her statement, and put the phone down without speaking.[141b]

This particular morning, Piggott arrived at Charles Street to be greeted at the door by Keiller's butler, Frazer, who was a character not unlike P G Wodehouse's Jeeves. Frazer took Piggott's hat and coat, and announced 'I must inform you that Mr Keiller's wife has left him, and Mr Keiller has locked himself in his room with his revolver. I have ascertained that the revolver is not loaded '.[142] After a great show of grief, spending two days locked in his room and eating all his meals in there, *O, he could still eat then!* Keiller emerged as though nothing had happened.

Less than a month later, Keiller was taken ill, and had to spend some time in a nursing home. Veronica was filled with remorse, and made tentative enquiries about her estranged husband, although not directly. When he came out of the nursing home early in 1934, they had lunch together at the Mayfair Hotel, where he told her that he was going abroad for some time because the doctor had said his nerves were in a bad state.

Veronica offered to go with him, hoping that if he agreed, and things went well, there might be some chance of a reconciliation. However, Keiller was already set on a course of his own choosing, and refused her offer, making his views quite plain. He travelled around Italy for a month, visiting Naples and Rome before going on to Pompeii.

At that time, one of his female acquaintances was Wyn Henderson, a former dancer who at one time managed Guggenheim's London gallery. Early in 1934, she had introduced him to Antonia White the novelist, who referred to him in writing as the Marmalade King. An entry in Antonia's diary described him as, 'A most odd man this: absolutely unscrupulous about other people's time, tastes or feelings. ... Yet I enjoy being with him in spite of egoism, bombast, self pity, merciless boredom. Full of vitality: has a definite charm and certainly an element of surprise. Exaggerated about everything – feelings, affections, suspicions. Forces everyone to take part in his life, whether digging up barrows, collecting cattle or skiing. Very generous, often mean. Not imaginative giver: yet can be extremely sensitive and shrewd. The most ruthless waster of other people's time that I know. Yet infects everyone with enthusiasm and obviously inspires passionate devotion in people who work for him'.[143] It is apparent from her writing that Keiller took more than a passing interest in her, and this was not to be the last time they met.

Another friend and associate of Keiller's, dating back to his military service during the war, was Rupert Gould. Gould was interested in the theory of the Sea Serpent, and had published a book about the subject in the early 1930s. Following continual sightings at Loch Ness of a 'sea monster', Gould was keen to investigate. Keiller suggested to him that he should visit Loch Ness, in order to collect evidence and examine the facts, and volunteered to bear the expense of the expedition. In the preface of the resulting book *The Loch Ness Monster and Others*,[144] Gould acknowledges Keiller as the 'onlie begetter' of the book. The volume is dedicated to Veronica, which suggests that Gould must have remained on friendly terms with her despite Keiller's own indifference.

30
EXPLORING NEW AVENUES

FOLLOWING A DISCUSSION with Keiller on the manuscripts of Stukeley's Avebury and Stonehenge surveys which Keiller had owned since 1924, and the prospects of general field work in Avebury, Piggott suggested that a restricted excavation, with reference to Stukeley's plans, might indicate the original course of the West Kennet Avenue, one of the stone avenues leading from the Avebury Circle.[145] Keiller showed great enthusiasm for this idea and plans were drawn up for April that same year. Excavation of the Avenue spanned two years, 1934-5, with the period between excavations being filled entirely with associated work. Digging began on land owned by James Peak-Garland, although later Keiller was to buy sections of the Avenue from local landowners. During the 1920s Keiller had booked all the rooms at the Red Lion in Avebury to accommodate his staff during the excavations. This now extended to Perry's Hotel, which was previously adjoined to the village shop and is now owned by the National Trust.

THE WEST KENNET AVENUE approaches Avebury stone circle from the south, being linked at its southernmost point to The Sanctuary, a possible ritual or ceremonial site of a contemporary age.

Many of the stones in the Avenue had been broken up in the eighteenth century,[146] and by the early 1900s only four stones remained upright with a total of thirteen still visible. Careful excavation uncovered a number of buried stones, and each was re-erected in its original place, being secured by a concrete base beneath the turf. Where a stone had been taken away or broken up, the position was marked with a concrete pillar after delicate field work had determined the presence of any finds. Having speculated on the method used by our ancestors to erect the stones, Keiller and Piggott reconstructed what was considered equivalent 'Prehistoric equipment', but using steel hawsers in place of ropes. It took a team of twelve men under the direction of a foreman five days to raise the first stone, which weighed approximately eight tons.

The excavation trenches were confined mainly to two strips just over 7m wide, with extensions if necessary to take in irregular spacings between the pairs of stone holes. At the outset of the first season an 'occupation' area was unexpectedly uncovered, and a major extension of 7m by 35m was made to the West of the excavation to include this area. Every time a new stone was discovered the work gangs lined up and a flag was raised to celebrate. As work progressed, a pattern began to emerge. The undressed (that is, in natural state, unlike Stonehenge where

Fig. 34. Raising a stone, West Kennet Avenue, 1934   *Alexander Keiller Museum, Avebury*

the shape of the 'dressed' sarsens was sculptured by human hand) sarsens had purposely been sited with contrasting shapes either side of the Avenue. These were designated Types A and B. Type A was generally a tall narrow pillar, whilst Type B roughly resembled a diamond lozenge shape. It was subsequently suggested that these represented male and female symbols, and that the monument was dedicated to a fertility cult. For a time Keiller thought that the Avebury stones were partially dressed, and it was considered by his employees heresy to challenge this statement in public.[147]

Other observations were made. The Avenue did not curve gracefully across the Downs as had been previously supposed, but ran in a series of straight lengths. The distance between opposing stones narrowed progressively on approach to the Circle at Avebury, presumably to make the appearance of the great henge more impressive to those following the route from the Sanctuary at Overton Hill to the Circle.

Four graves were discovered, two with fragmentary beakers.[148] In one of these the arms of the skeleton were crossed and the hands laid on the shoulders.

During the first season the combined length of the trenches was something over half a mile, with various gangs working on different tasks. Keiller listed the excavating gang, the concreting gang, the re-filling gang, the re-turfing gang, and so on. It would have been an impossible task to refill and returf such a vast area satisfactorily in one go afterwards, so each section was refilled and re-turfed within – at the outside – a week of completion of the concreting work. This considerable feat forced Keiller to let the moor at Morven for the shooting season, not only because he did not have the time to travel up to Scotland, but also to help finance the excavation. He deemed it '..better to put up eleven stones than bring down eleven brace to one's own gun every drive of the year'.[149]

Fig. 35. Large-scale excavations, West Kennet Avenue, Avebury, Wiltshire, 1934
Alexander Keiller Museum, Avebury

Evidence of human occupation came to light half a mile outside the henge on the course of the Avenue, although there was no evidence of dwellings or structures. Pottery sherds, animal bones and pits located the site where perhaps the builders of the Avenue had camped during the course of their monumental task. Within this area Keiller put a flat topped concrete pillar (or *stela*),[150] as opposed to the pyramid-topped pillars denoting missing stones. Looking at the natural progression and route of the Avenue, it followed that a stone should have been placed in this position. It was not. The reason why one stone was omitted in an otherwise precise sequence remains a mystery.

In all, during two seasons, Keiller uncovered the original location of 53 missing megaliths, although only 27 stones remained in these locations to be re-erected, or, as with Mrs Cunnington's stone,[151] reset. Their missing counterparts were marked by *stelae* so to give a full picture of that section of the original Avenue. Keiller told a friend that the sound of the cement mixer pounding was the most beautiful sound in the world, knowing that each newly unearthed stone would be fixed in her hole and in three thousand years she would still be standing.[152]

Really?

72

Many of the Windmill Hill team had returned to assist with the new excavations. Young was employed as foreman, and of course this time the team was strengthened by the presence of Stuart Piggott. Other new faces appeared, among them Barbara Laidler, a young archaeologist,[153] Doris Emerson Chapman, who was employed to make drawings of all the Avebury stones, and for a week whilst visiting his friend Young, Thurstan Shaw.[154] Keiller also interviewed and employed a new secretary, Mrs Sorel-Taylour. Initially she was employed as his private secretary at Charles Street and then in Avebury, but his new archaeological secretary did not like the countryside, and left. Sorel-Taylour was then made secretary on both counts, but did not have any active involvement in the archaeology.

31
DECREE ABSOLUTE

FOLLOWING A TELEPHONE CONVERSATION with Dorothy Liddell in the summer of 1934, when Dorothy conveyed to Keiller how miserable her sister had been since his abrupt rejection, Keiller relented and offered to meet up with his wife.

On his suggestion they met at a halfway point between Sherfield and Avebury, in Savernake Forest. Veronica was delighted by the invitation, and on that summer's day made her way to the forest full of anticipation. Knowing from experience that she must tread carefully, she chose her words with great deliberation, and asked him if there was any chance at all that she could return to London and live with him. Keiller would have none of it, and completely lost his temper, terminating the meeting less than ten minutes after he had arrived, and leaving Veronica with her hopes well and truly shattered.[155]

As if to make his position entirely clear, within weeks Keiller sent a letter to Veronica stating that he had spent the night of the 3rd June at the Connaught Hotel in London with Mary Hanley, one of the circle of friends from whom Veronica had been excluded back at the start of their marital problems.

As with his previous wife, Keiller most graciously supplied a hotel bill for the night in question with the names Mr & Mrs Keiller thereon. Veronica made enquiries to confirm the details on the bill, and as a result a divorce petition was served to Keiller at Charles Street in the presence of Stuart Piggott.

By November the case was brought to court, once more in Scotland, and a succession of witnesses from the Connaught Hotel were presented in order to exercise their impeccable memories as regard to the night of the alleged adultery.

The marriage was dissolved, with a small settlement for Veronica, although even in court she maintained that she would never lose her affection for him. She remarried in 1937, and died in South Africa in 1964.[156]

32
A VISION OF AVEBURY

THE RETURN TO AVEBURY heralded a new phase in Keiller's life. Once again he was swept under the spell, and late one night he awoke Piggott in the Red Lion at Avebury to announce that he had decided to buy as much of the Avenue and Avebury as was possible and devote his life to its excavation and restoration.[157]   One of his first purchases was seven acres containing a portion of the West Kennet Avenue, at a cost of £500.

He was gripped by the vision of Avebury as it once had been, and his dream was to see the village moved out of the Stone Circle in order to restore the monument to its original splendour. Theory aside he referred to the stones as she, romanticising that 'each one would look out as far as she could see, with only green hills around her'.[158]

During the second season of the Avenue excavation, which began on June 4 and lasted four months in 1935, Keiller was able to procure a fourteen year lease on the Manor House in Avebury. In September he transferred his London staff and personal belongings to the Manor. His large collection of Egyptian artefacts, which included canopic jars, ancient glass and ushabti figures were stored at a warehouse in London together with an extensive collection of flint implements from all over

Fig. 36. Avebury Manor, South Front, in Keiller's time. The two adjacent lower gable windows were Keiller's bedroom and dressing room. *Alexander Keiller Museum, Avebury*

the world. In a letter to Passmore he states, '..We shall move into the Manor ourselves at the beginning of September "our guids and chattellis having preceded us", after which it is a pleasant thought that we will not again need to leave North Wiltshire for some years to come – at least I hope not; unless, indeed, perhaps the Cunningtons prevail upon the Chief Constable to have us expelled from the county!..'[159]

He wrote to Norrington, 'Last year, as you may have heard, I was excavating the megalithic avenue leading from Overton Hill to the Avebury circle, and the next twelve years will be spent in completing this task, and also dealing, I trust adequately, with the circle as a whole, identifying all stone holes and re-erecting fallen megaliths or those discovered buried, the existence of which has hitherto been unsuspected.[160]

One of his new staff, an artist named Doris Emerson Chapman, set up a business with Keiller whereby he took a photograph of clients and she painted a portrait from the photograph. It is not known how long this arrangement lasted, but the business relationship progressed rapidly to a personal level, and when Keiller moved to the Manor at Avebury, Doris Chapman accompanied him as 'Mistress in Residence'.[161]

He apparently suffered some financial loss in a 'monstrous crash' during this period, although it can only have mildly dented his fortune, as he began to realise his dream of buying Avebury. Nevertheless he said that he only continued lunching at his old haunts to keep a stiff upper lip, and that Doris, having grown out of her previous year's evening dresses, could not afford a new one, and had to buy her jewellery at Woolworths.[162]

In apparent conflict with this statement, they had a holiday together in France following the move to Avebury, where Keiller took some photographs of various Palaeolithic sculptures in the rock shelter of Cap Blanc, and other local archaeological sites, copies of which were presented to the British Museum and also the Natural Museum at St. Germain. A paper was published in *Antiquity* in 1936 under their joint names entitled 'The Rock Shelter at Cap Blanc'.[163]

He renewed his acquaintance with Antonia White. She complained of him making the usual scene over the mixing of his martini cocktail, and that he constantly drew attention to his false teeth even though she was sure he had them when he was first introduced to her. According to her diaries she was never his mistress, and although she had heard that he was reputed to be a sadist she considered him the most sentimental man she had ever known. This view was to change rapidly when, behind drawn curtains in Berkeley Square, Keiller asked her to climb into a laundry basket wearing nothing but a mackintosh so that he could poke her through the wicker work with an umbrella.[164]   When she later confided in Wyn Henderson about this episode, Wyn, who was 'enormously fat and always short of money ...

had retorted, "If he can find a large enough basket, and pay enough money, I'll do it for him!"[164a]

how nicely put!

This unusual approach does not seem to have deterred his mistresses, if he indeed pursued this avenue with all of them, although might point to the reason why they were mostly transient.

It was during the mid-'30s that one of Keiller's most bizarre sexual phases took place. He and a small group of like-minded gentlemen would meet for drinks at a club, following which they would adjourn to a flat in South London where a young lady waited for them. Each of the men would take turns with the woman in what was a curiously formal and ritualistic act of sexual intercourse. Afterwards, when the men had gone their separate ways, they would later correspond with each other discussing intimately the parts of the ritual which excited them most.[164b] Keiller in his own words said, 'I have, at different times in my life, made studies, more or less cursory and sometimes merely superficial, of various branches of the erotic impulse ...'.[165] Every aspect of life he embraced with enthusiasm, and this was no exception!

That explains him + Piggott, then + his comment that "Someone ought really to tell Peggy" but no one did

33
THE MORVEN INSTITUTE

NINETEEN-THIRTY-SIX was a busy and eventful year for Keiller. He bought the Parish Allotments at Avebury from the Parish Council, the first of several land acquisitions.

On January 28th he attended the funeral of King George V, taking photographs which he decided to have made into small memorial albums for each of the party who was present with him on the occasion. He instructed his photographic specialist at the Wallace Heaton company to have each booklet bound in his customary brown leather, and a copy sent to Miss Chapman, Miss Laidler, Miss Hebden, Miss S. Lockett, and Mr and Mrs Holmes. Each book contained a photographic reproduction of his 'invitation' to the funeral.[166]

He caught a slight chill whilst watching the procession, although this did not deter him from attending the Harvey-Petersen fight the following evening, where he had a ringside seat.[167] Throughout February he was laid low by this chill which became progressively worse, and it was only at the beginning of March that he was back on his feet again 'albeit shakily'.

As far as Avebury was concerned, Keiller was intrigued by the 'Ringstone', which had stood within the southern inner 'circle' and was represented in Stukeley's eighteenth-century plans and etchings, which Keiller possessed. Some of these now

where are these?

form a part of the Alexander Keiller Collection at the Bodleian Library, and were donated shortly before his death in 1955.

Whilst in Avebury that spring he examined the etchings and selected two which showed the Ringstone. From these he chose two identifiable points in each and took them as terminal positions on imaginary base lines. These gave him the possible location on paper of the 'Ringstone', and in practice on reaching this place, Keiller's assistant 'found that he was standing in a hollow, almost certainly representing a stone hole'. Keiller deemed this a 'very remarkable tribute to the accuracy of ... Stukeley's draughtsmanship'.[168]

The Manor at Avebury became headquarters for the Morven Institute of Archaeological Research which had been registered as a business name by Keiller in June of 1935. In November 1936 he described the Institute as follows...

'The MIAR takes its territorial designation from Morven on Deeside in Aberdeenshire, which for many years formed, and indeed still forms, the headquarters of the Institute in Scotland, particularly for the work carried out by myself, and by members of my field working staff during the last twenty years in reference to megalithic monuments of North-East Scotland. The English headquarters of the Institute was previously at 4, Charles Street, Berkeley Square, where was situated the Institute's Museum, which included among other items, the whole of the finds – essential as regards any study of the Neolithic period in Britain – from Windmill Hill ...

... In view of the fact that members of the Institute will be engaged on excavation and research work, in connection with the Avebury Complex, for at least the next twelve years to come, it was considered desirable to transfer the English headquarters of the Institute from London to the district of Avebury itself, to which end ... Mr Piggott, myself and members of the staff, have taken up our residence in the vicinity of Avebury.

The Morven Institute is composed of a certain number of selected professional archaeologists, chosen on account of their experience, or other qualifications, in connection with special branches of archaeological research. ... Although the library of the Institute has been arranged and in use here since the beginning of last May [1936], while the same applies to such offices as the Map Room, and Drawing Office, other contents of the Museum have not yet been transferred from London, on account of the delay occasioned by alterations to the building destined for their housing.'[169]

As regards Morven, he explained the choice of name for the Institute by saying that it was very important to him. He had been brought up in Morven, and had spent much of his life there. He might be prejudiced, but he thought 'that

Morven represents one of the most beautiful parts of the whole of the North of Scotland' during every season of the year'.[170]

It is ironic that his involvement with Avebury took him even further away from Scotland, as increasing commitments kept him away from his family home.

In Spring of 1936 he travelled to New York with Hugo Eckner on the 'Hindenburg' Zeppelin 129 airship. Whilst on the trip he suggested to Eckner, the designer, that the airship could be used for a grandiose archaeological air survey. He told Piggott the airship was 'so slow and large that you could plot sites straight on to six-inch maps – and it's even got a bar!'.[171] He spent only seven hours in America during the trip, which he said was 'adequate'.

His New Year greeting card the following January boasted a photo taken 'from the Hindenburg, somewhere over the Atlantic'.[172] To have one of his own photographs as the focal point of his cards was by no means unusual. Other interesting (though not terribly festive) examples were pictures of 'Felstead', the canine skeleton discovered on Windmill Hill in 1928, and 'Duffine', the goat excavated in 1929.

34
PASTURES NEW

O N KEILLER'S RETURN to England, and Avebury, he and Piggott decided that it would be a good idea to write a short and 'much needed' guide book concerning the archaeological features in and around Avebury.[173] Keiller wrote to Passmore asking for his assistance on this project since he considered that there was no man in Wiltshire who knew more about the field archaeology of the area than Passmore.

This idea was put to one side temporarily when the Morven Institute was asked by the Surrey Archaeological Society to supervise the excavation of the Badshot Lea Long Barrow near Farnham in Surrey.[174] Keiller and Piggott were joint directors, and it was an opportunity for the Institute to survey the landscape for Prehistoric evidence.

Following his land purchases and in line with his ambition to return Avebury to her former splendour, Keiller ordered a survey of the monument, which emphasised the fact that it was 'the national archaeological disgrace of Britain'.[175] Within the henge banks, and close to the Cove amongst the more sturdy and aesthetic dwellings in the village, lay a jumble of pigsties, derelict corrugated buildings, crumbling cottages, and an old garage which was in need of renovation. The whole area was overgrown with shrubs and trees, and the remaining stones of the Circle

< 'Stuart Piggott is a slimy toad " written in Passmore notebook DM.

78

were overshadowed by indiscriminate building.

On purchasing certain plots and buildings Keiller set about removing unsightly encumbrances and in some cases replacing them. An arrangement with Rawlins involving an exchange of land, meant that a new garage was eventually built outside the Circle and away from the monument itself. This can still be seen today on approach from the northern side on the main road through the village. *see her book publ 1999*

An explosives expert was hired to deal with the problem of removing trunk roots after the trees had been felled. Owing to his expertise in this field little damage was done to the monument. It was during this procedure that Stuart Piggott was hit on the head by a lump of flying debris, and Keiller commented, 'The excavations had to be held up intermittently while tree stumps were blasted out of the side of the ditch. With the new methods now being employed, large tree stumps were blown right over the vallum and fell in the paddock. A smaller portion fell through the roof of one of Peak-Garland's cowsheds, while a shrapnel of timber fell into his pig field. Finally, to my intense delight, a piece of timber descended vertically on to the top of Stuart's [Piggott's] head. It is well, I think, for these youngsters to experience some of the horrors which we veterans underwent, with relative cheerfulness, in the

Fig. 37. Blowing up tree stumps at Avebury Henge to clear the area for excavation and restoration *Alexander Keiller Museum, Avebury*

79

Ypres salient in 1915'.[176]

35
PETRIFIED STONES

ON OCTOBER 30th 1936, the South-West Sub-Committee for the Petrological Identification of Stone Implements was set up, with Keiller as Chairman and Stuart Piggott as Secretary. Petrological Identification involves taking a thin section of a specimen to examine under a microscope, with the hope of matching the rock to a known outcrop. In the case of stone implements such as stone axes or mace heads, which have been ground or polished, superficial examination cannot give a precise enough picture, and thin sectioning is the only accurate method of discovering the origins of the stone.

Keiller had been interested in this line of research since the days of his early fieldwork in Aberdeenshire. When excavating at Windmill Hill he sent specimens to H. H. Thomas of the Geological Survey, who had earlier identified the source of the bluestones at Stonehenge through the same method. Most of the Windmill Hill specimens were found to come from North Wales, with some being 'augite granophyre' which is only to be found at Graig Lwyd in Gwynedd, where large prehistoric quarries were known to exist, although a small proportion were from further afield. Through this study of the specimens, and subsequent results, Keiller was able to throw light on the cultural connections in Neolithic times between Wiltshire and North Wales.

Charles Drew, who had excavated with Keiller and Piggott at Thickthorn Down in 1933, was now in 1936 Curator of the Dorchester Museum. He was also interested in this field, and together with Keiller instigated the formation of this new 'Petrological Identification of Stone Implements Sub-Committee' which was organised through the Morven Institute, by the South West Group of Museums. As well as Keiller, Piggott and Drew, other members elected at this first meeting included Gray, Dr F. S. Wallis and Mrs E. M. Clifford. The functions of the committee were to collate work already carried out by other researchers in this field, to take thin sections from suitable specimens and compare the results of petrological analyses. Records were to be compiled by means of fully documented and illustrated cards, to be available for other researchers to study, and from time to time interim reports would be published to update members on progress. In 1945, through the Council for British Archaeology, the group became a national enterprise, thus enabling this important and hitherto unrecognised line of research to continue.[177]

36
LANHILL

THE FIRST WEEK IN OCTOBER brought an urgent telephone call from A. D. Passmore asking if Keiller and the M.I.A.R. would undertake an excavation which it was necessary to commence first thing on the following morning. The excavation represented an extreme archaeological rarity, being the untouched chamber of a Neolithic burial mound. The location was Lanhill, near Chippenham in Wiltshire.

Passmore had been supervising the renewal of the railings next to a long barrow when he noticed that the North-West corner of the mound was undisturbed. Previously Cunnington had excavated a chamber on the Southern side of the Barrow. The possibility of a burial chamber intact within the mound prompted further investigation. As it was, the chamber was capped with a large stone over two yards long and a little over one and a half yards wide. The stone was only a few inches thick, and broken into four parts. Lifting one of these fragments, Passmore discovered a chamber underneath, and knew that prompt excavation was required. Passmore reluctantly replaced the stone and hurried off to enlist the help of the M.I.A.R., who were only too willing to assist.

The remains of eight individuals were found, ranging from a young adolescent to an 'aged' female. One of the skulls was absent, as were several limbs from three of the other individuals. Doris Chapman, now an M.I.A.R. member, put her artistic

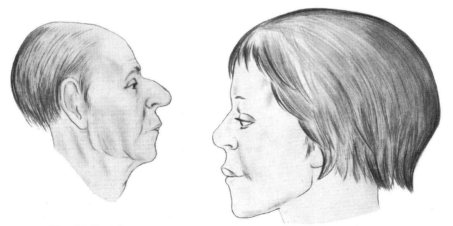

Fig. 38. Facial reconstructions of Lanhill skulls, by Doris Chapman
Alexander Keiller Museum, Avebury

background to good use by producing facial reconstructions on paper of four of the skulls. These were printed by the M.I.A.R. with the excavation report, also appearing in the *Proceedings of the Prehistoric Society* 1938.[178]

Keiller had to break off his excavation work to travel to London in order to give a lecture to the Society of Antiquaries on his work at Avebury.

It was perhaps on this visit to town that Keiller dined out with old acquaintances, writing to Piggott after one occasion, 'Sing Ho! for the Brushwood Boy! No sooner had I come to London than I met a Davey Fergusson whose name is Paaaul[sic]. He was introduced to me while I was dining with some friends, and I am given to understand that the effect upon me was electric and unexpected; for the rest of the meal even the waiters considered that for once I was very drunk, and was showing it intermittently by bursting into snatches of song while my expression was apparently ecstatic ... His eyes are lustrous, and I am told he sews divinely; he is indeed, a mere outsider...'[179]

The remarks are on the whole cryptic, but suggest, as in other surviving correspondence, that he was not indifferent to all of his male associates.

we know

37
OF LOCAL INTEREST

THE CLOSE OF THE YEAR saw Keiller still busily involved in plans for the excavation of the North-Western sector of the Circle at Avebury. In December he wrote to Norrington at the Clarendon Press, saying that his secretary had pointed out to him that in four days of the preceding week he had dictated (by dictaphone) no less than 193 letters. These were all dictated outside normal working hours.[180]

This was by no means an unusual occurrence and in matter of fact, several of these letters were likely to be to the same person. He began a number system when writing to certain people, such as his photographic adviser, so that they could keep track of the order of his letters, as it was not unknown for him to write as often as ten times a day on various matters.

As complicated as his letters often were, he liked them to be correct, and replying to a less than perfect example, he noted, 'You ought not to be writing to me as "A Keiller, Esq, M A" since I have no claim to any degrees suggesting learning of any description. It is always a little galling to me that although otherwise intelligent foreigners frequently address Stuart Piggott as "Professor Piggott", or "Dr Piggott", or even 'Dr Professor Piggott", such persons only write to me as "Sir Keiller', or on one notorious occasion,"My Lord Keiller".[181]

In December, Keiller went up to London for a meeting of the Prehistoric Society. Young had travelled up in advance, and visited the British Museum to see two plaster casts of decorated surfaces from the West Kennet Avenue stones, that had been set up in the main entrance hall.[182]   He noted that the museum had '...outlined the ... sculptured markings wrongly on both casts and painted extra lines with loops without having the faintest reason for doing so... thus ruining them completely...'.[183]   He added that 'Mr Keiller will go clean mad when he sees them', which of course he did, and Young received a telegram from Keiller saying that the casts had been removed from the exhibition. The matter was dealt with by no less than Reginald Smith, himself.

From the third of January 1937 onwards, in what must have been bitterly cold conditions, Keiller's team were engaged in the titanic task of re-excavating every cutting excavated on Windmill Hill between 1925 and 1929 inclusive, 'in order that we might returf the whole flush on to the virgin chalk, thus preserving for students in particular and for the general public ... the appearance of ... the type-site of the Neolithic 'A' period in Britain ... preserving the ditches in their pristine entirety, although, of course, banks have been ploughed away'.[184]

A young Leslie Grinsell was at that time working in a London branch of Barclays Bank whilst devoting his spare time to fieldwork, principally on barrows in Wessex. Keiller offered to pay his bank salary for up to four weeks of each year if he could be released from the bank to do that much more fieldwork. Grinsell's bank manager was agreeable but the Staff Manager replied that he was unable to accede to Mr Keiller's request.[185] It was not until later in life that Grinsell was able to dedicate his life to the pursuit of archaeological knowledge.

Spending most of his time in Avebury, Keiller became to some degree involved in local activities. He was elected as a member of the Selection Committee of the Avebury Football Club, and invited to the first match of the season which was against a village 'with the typically English name of Bradenstoke-cum-clack'.[186]

A little further afield in Wroughton he part financed a speedway course just outside the village. Keiller's driver Philip Withil was involved with the racing, and his mechanic Harold Jarman who lived in Wroughton was official examiner of vehicles at speedway events.[187]

To the local people, although a generous patron and provider of much needed employment, Keiller must have seemed an eccentric character. Dressed perhaps in a deer-stalker cap, loud check shirt and tweeds, or his M.I.A.R. blazer and battered straw hat bearing Windmill Hill colours (green and white), he would walk amongst his 'crew' on site, striding solid and self-possessed from one work team to another. Describing himself once as the Captain of a ship whilst on site, with the workers as his shipmates, he was a force to be reckoned with.[188]

A daughter of Mr Perry, who owned the hotel in the village, recalls him standing on a box shouting orders at his staff through a megaphone, so that his instructions might be heard by everyone present.[189] He was a man of moods, and it was deemed unwise to argue against him, although if left to his own devices he would often modify his views. According to those who knew him, he was blessed with a great natural intelligence.

He was a collector of unusual things, from rare East European stamps to Cow Creamer jugs. After his death, his widow gave to the Stoke-on-Trent Museum a collection of 666 Cow Creamers, which make up the Keiller Collection there. Jane Lees, a resident of Avebury, recalled how he pleaded with her mother in the 1930s to sell him a cream jug which sat on her dresser. His generous offer was refused, and the jug still sits today on the dresser, silent proof that money cannot buy everything![190]

One of his eccentricities, at a time when it was en vogue to carry a silver cigarette case, was to keep his Russian cigarettes in a battered old tin from which all the engraving had been worn away.[191] He was very much a product of his public school education and upbringing, but at the same time liked to stand out from the crowd.

Fig. 39. The Map Room, in a neat and orderly fashion, Avebury Manor
Alexander Keiller Museum, Avebury

Fig. 40. 'The Mousetrap' dressing-room, Avebury Manor
Alexander Keiller Museum, Avebury

It was in 1937 that Keiller employed a temporary secretary, Miss Elizabeth Neal, who advertised in *The Times* following her return from Africa, 'Temporary Lady requires Secretarial Position'. Keiller's permanent secretary was in hospital, and Keiller took on Miss Neal, calling her 'TL', telling her that she was given an interview because he wanted to see what a 'Temporary Lady' looked like. She stayed in the secretary's cottage in the Manor drive, and her meals were brought over from the Manor. She remembers him as 'a wonderful employer, very generous and kind, with a wonderful sense of humour'.[192]

As though to confirm his commitment to Avebury, Keiller concluded negotiations with the owner of the Manor and bought the house with all associated buildings outright. Plans were put in hand to convert the racquets court for use as a museum although at a later date this location was changed to the stable block owing to the difficulty in public access to the former site, and parts of the house which had fallen into disrepair were soon restored. The library which had been added to the house in the early 1900s by its previous owner Colonel Jenner, was filled with Keiller's considerable collection of books.

The Map Room in the East Wing was converted to be as it was in London, the Brown Room. Denis Grant King, who visited the following year noted that 'everything was brown -- brown velvet curtains, brown window seats, brown carpet, and brown leather covered walls'.[193] He did not mention the leather stools-cum-waste paper baskets, but we must assume that they also had made the journey from London.

Keiller's own rooms on the top floor were sparsely furnished, a stark contrast of dark wood and bare floor boards with a scattering of animal rugs. His dressing room he fondly called the 'Mouse Trap'. In his own words he described this as his 'private sanctum - the outstanding characteristic of which is that it is equipped with that indescribable degree of personal discomfort which can only come from exclusively period furniture of the middle of the XVI century ...'.[193a] His study was a neat and orderly room, a reflection of his personal obsession with detail.

38
A CIRCLE OF STONES

AVEBURY STONE CIRCLE is surrounded by a large bank and ditch, that is, a henge monument. The bank of the henge is three quarters of a mile in circumference, and originally would have risen 50ft above the base of the ditch. The outer circle of stones encloses over 28 acres, and there are two inner circles. The Northern inner circle includes the Cove, and the Southern holds the Z stones and the site of the Obelisk.

Aubrey was the first to visit Avebury in 1649, followed by Pepys in 1668, and they would likely have seen more of the circles than Stukeley did in the 1720s when destruction of the stones had been ongoing for over a decade. Curiously, the stone circle we see today is a good deal different to the circle Pepys and Stukeley observed, for many of the stones re-erected in the 1930s by Keiller had been buried over three centuries before Pepys visited the site.

In Spring 1937, restoration and excavation work began on the stone circle within the North Western sector, which includes the great Diamond or Swindon stone. This stone itself was vastly encumbered by trees and overgrown with bracken, and the task to clear all of this in order to undertake archaeological work was no small feat. In a letter to Ormsby-Gore of H. M. Office of Works in London, Keiller expressed his hopes that at the conclusion of the season's excavation work this quadrant of the circle would represent 'something of a show house, whilst work is in progress, for potential subscribers to realise the extent of reconstruction which is still possible'.[194]

Some of the stones lay over a metre below the surface. Eight stones in all were unearthed and raised in their original stone holes. As at the West Kennet

Avenue, concrete pillars were used to denote where a missing stone had once stood. Careful excavation of the area east of the Diamond stone, which had always been considered merely the historic route of the Swindon road, proved that it had been a genuine entrance to the Circle left as a causeway when surrounding chalk had been hacked away with antler picks to create the ditch surrounding the monument.

Fig. 41. Excavations of the North-West sector of Avebury Stone Circle, 1937. In the foreground a concrete *stela*; to the left and centre newly erected megaliths; to the right a gang returfing the bank   *Alexander Keiller Museum, Avebury*

A curious discovery was the presence of three stoneholes, one of which by nature of its position close to the Diamond stone could not possibly have held a stone of any great height or magnitude at the same time as the Diamond stone stood. Keiller speculated that the three stoneholes represented a third circle, but this is unsubstantiated, although the centre of such a circle would have lain on precisely the same axis as the centres of the southern and central interior settings. Also the diameter of the 'circle' was, within a couple of feet, identical to that of the other two circles. It remains a possibility that this 'third circle' may have existed, but if so the three stones must have been removed before the commencement of a later phase of construction which included the Great Circle, and the bank and ditch (henge). Nearly thirty years later, Piggott returned to Avebury to look for other stone holes in the 'third circle' but none were found. *What would magnetometers show?*

87

Fig. 42. Stuart Piggott and Doris Chapman at work   *Alexander Keiller Museum, Avebury*

At the outset of this first season, only four stones in the sector were standing with a further four visible on the ground. On completion twelve stones stood in the same setting as had been chosen for them 4000 years previously. Some of the stones had been cracked and damaged during attempts to break them up for use in the village as building stone. This was done by setting straw in pits and then toppling the stone into the pit. The straw was then set on fire, and when the stone was hot, water was poured onto it before breaking it up with a sledge hammer. Much of this was done in Stukeley's day as a two-fold exercise to clear the land for cultivation and provide local building stone. Some of these attempts were less than successful and the results were simply left where they lay. Keiller repaired the damaged stones as well as he was able with the use of non-corrosive metal rods, some of these megaliths being quite apparent in present day by their awkward and incomplete shape.

Perhaps due to the high profile publicity surrounding the excavation work, and a certain degree of national embarrassment at the state of neglect at a monument of major historic importance, a scheme was initiated by Ormsby-Gore of the Office of Works to raise money to buy the land around Avebury. Keiller was involved peripherally with the scheme, and was consulted about some of the resulting plans, although he thought it was locally considered as a 'dead letter' because of the 'archaeologists are behind it all to the detriment of local inhabitants' attitude.[195]

His personal opinion of the scheme was somewhat derisive. As late as 1939, owing to his financial situation, he told Awdry, 'I am afraid that independently I shall not be able to complete the task which I have regarded as a duty, and have undertaken as such ...[ref: the restoration of the circle]. Looking at the brighter side of the matter, however, the Circle of Avebury and the more important part of the West Kennet Avenue, is at least preserved for the nation for all time, which, to put it cruelly bluntly, is more than the Avebury Preservation Scheme has hitherto achieved in so far as even a square yard of territory is concerned, and actually represents more than the Avebury Preservation Scheme could ever have achieved'.[196] The aim of the Avebury Preservation Scheme was to raise the sum of £11,000 in order to secure the future of Avebury by preventing any undesirable development of countryside. The money was raised and the land duly presented to the National Trust.

*When ?
see p 107*

Of his continuing work at Avebury, and summing up his feelings, Keiller said, 'I am not going to deny that there are occasions when I feel a restless resentment at my self-enforced concentration upon the "Avebury Complex"; occasions when the call of archaeology in its wider sense makes itself felt ... but these I quell with the assistance of my sincere belief that this work must be carried out ... coupled with my conviction that if I do not carry it out, judging by the example of past centuries, no-one else is likely to do so, and at any rate, merits or qualifications apart, no-one with so wholehearted and innate a love of the stones themselves as I, myself, feel.'[197]

39
THE MUSEUM AT AVEBURY

POST-EXCAVATION WORK continued throughout the winter months, and during the spring of 1938, the entire contents of Keiller's private museum at Charles Street were transported to the newly refurbished stable block at Avebury in the grounds of the Manor. Proceedings were overshadowed by the fact that Dorothy Liddell was lying dangerously ill at her home in Stratfield Turgis. She had been unwell since the previous October.

Young and Stuart Piggott helped to put the finishing touches to the Museum, which displayed many of the Windmill Hill and West Kennet Avenue finds. Amongst the later articles uncovered during the excavations was a broken 'Keiller' marmalade jar which was included by Piggott in the section displaying post-Neolithic evidence, something which Keiller found highly amusing on his inspection of the display.[198]

The Museum was duly opened at 3pm on June 1st, and this event was reported upon in *The Times* on June 6. A quote from a speech read by T. D. Kendrick of the British Museum declared that 'No archaeologist had ever fought a giant with the grim single-handed thoroughness with which Keiller was then wrestling with Avebury. In the British Museum, they were beginning to realise the short-comings of excavations that were not really complete. The results of these remained under suspicion, but at Avebury there were no such dangers for Mr Keiller had proceeded with painstaking thoroughness, and although he might not know, had attained the position of the foremost field archaeologist in Britain'.[199]

Keiller, replying, thanked everyone who had done so much for the museum, most especially his sister-in-law Dorothy Liddell who had died the previous week. He wanted to think of the Museum as a tribute to her work. Some of the items on display were entirely due to her, such as the demonstration of the use of various bird and small animal bones to create patterns on Neolithic pottery. An established archaeologist, she had devoted much time to the Windmill Hill seasons and post-excavation research.

On opening the museum, Keiller said that the collection was not complete but he hoped that it never would be, as it represented the results of the M.I.A.R.'s continuing work at Avebury. During the first five months over 6000 visitors passed through the doors of the museum.

Fig. 43. Avebury Museum exterior, 1954   *Alexander Keiller Museum, Avebury*

Fig. 44. Avebury Museum interior, 1954, with Young and Spackman
Alexander Keiller Museum, Avebury

40
THE GLASS SLIPPER

L ESS THAN A WEEK later work began on clearing the South-West sector of the Circle in preparation for the year's excavation. The blacksmith's shop was removed, and all the silt and rubbish taken from the ditch with the intention of eventually exposing the natural chalk.

The outline of the initial sections was laid out on Friday June 10th, and excavation commenced four days later. In this sector only one stone was standing and a further three remained visible. Keiller referred to this sector as the 'Cinderella' of Avebury because of the apparent lack of stones.

During the first ten days of the excavations no fewer than five unsuspected buried stones were uncovered, as well as, at the eastern end, a stonehole and a burning destruction pit. At the end of the year Keiller hoped to have at least six standing stones in line, and a total of eleven standing when only one had stood before.

Fig. 45. The South-West sector of Avebury Stone Circle prior to excavation, 1938
Alexander Keiller Museum, Avebury

According to an acquaintance of Keiller's at that time, the well known spiritualist, Edith Olivier, assisted Keiller in her own way by 'sensing' where the next stone was to be found, a method about which Keiller kept an open mind.[200]

It was during this time that Denis Grant King arrived in Avebury, hoping to become a part of the excavation team. King was a skilled artist, adept at sketching quickly and accurately, and this talent brought him to Keiller's attention. He kept a diary from the day of his arrival in Avebury, and his amusing observations are interspersed with small ink sketches. His first impression of Keiller is recorded in his diary as follows: ' ... Tall, well built man, brown hair and good shaped head, and an interesting somewhat furrowed face. He looks distinguished and speaks with distinction. His conversation like his letter writing is voluminous; his sentences almost of the periodic type. He speaks of course with decision and confidence, but occasionally his 'R's' seem appropriate [sic] to 'W's'.[201]

On the fifteenth day of excavation, when one of the buried stones was lifted, a remarkable discovery was made. Pressed against the side of the burial pit of the newly discovered stone was a skeleton. At first this find was thought to be of one of the Neolithic builders of the Great Circle, but after photographing the skeleton and carefully recording its position, the bones were lifted one by one to reveal three silver coins dating back to the fourteenth century, a bodkin and a pair of scissors, suggesting to Keiller that the man had been a tailor or barber-surgeon during the Middle Ages.

92

Fig. 46. The South-West sector of Avebury Stone Circle post-excavation, 1939
Alexander Keiller Museum, Avebury

This was the first time anyone had considered that the stones may have been buried before Stukeley's time.It was later assumed that the 'barber-surgeon' must have been helping with the burial of these 'pagan' stones, perhaps pressed into assistance by local representatives of the church, when the stone fell upon him and he was crushed. Surprisingly his skull was still intact, and Doris Chapman was able to sketch it in order to create a facial reconstruction.

The haste of this operation was due to Keiller's worry that the local Roman Catholic Priest, backed by a certain section of public opinion, may have wished to re-inter the 'corpse', posing the difficult question in Keiller's mind to whether the excavation staff should send a wreath or not.[202] *Ha ha*

This dilemma was not necessary, for the bones were soon dispatched to Dr Cave at the Royal College of Surgeons in London following approval from the coroner, for further investigation, whilst the scissors and bodkin were sent to Plenderleath for examination and treatment for preservation. Keiller was a keen advocate of specialist analysis, a practice which he felt had previously been much overlooked. *✓✓*

The barber-surgeon's scissors can now be seen on display at the Museum in Avebury, though the skeleton was sadly destroyed during the London Blitz in the 1940s. *No – found by mike Pitts in Nat. Hist. Mus, 1999 while looking for something else (as usual)*

At this point in the excavation, Keiller longed to discover just one more buried stone, the existence of which was not hitherto suspected, so that he would

93

above left Fig. 47. Dennis Grant King's cartoon sketch of the South-East sector excavation
in progress, 1939 (© *Margaret Nurse*)
below left Fig. 48. Stuart Piggott holding the Barber-Surgeon's skull, on site, Avebury,
1938 *Alexander Keiller Museum, Avebury*
above Fig. 49. Turfing the ditch in the South-West sector, 1938 *Alexander Keiller
Museum, Avebury*

be able to claim at the end of the season that he had completed the first half of the
Outer Circle of Avebury. This included confirmed locations of those stones under
houses, roads, outbuildings, gardens and so forth.[203]

Restoration of the sector continued until the end of November. Keiller did
find a further two buried stones, fulfilling his ambition, and leaving for future
generations the most complete quadrant of the Great Circle. The Cinderella of
Avebury was at last permitted to go to the Ball!

41
DORIS EMERSON CHAPMAN

IN SEPTEMBER, Keiller wrote to Norrington at the Clarendon Press in Oxford
requesting an interview for Doris Chapman with regard to the publication of a
book. He described her as 'one of the best, as well as one of the most intelligent, not
to say intellectual, assistants that I have ever had'. Leaving behind her career as an

artist she had become an acknowledged authority on megalithic monuments, although in recent years she had specialised in anthropology, most notably with the facial reconstructions of specimens of prehistoric races, and this was the intended subject matter of the book. Her work was considered so accurate that it attracted the attention of Scotland Yard, who were interested in using her skills should it be necessary in a case.[204] Norrington replied politely, but stated that the work was too much of a specialist field to be published on its own merit, although the illustrations would be more than adequate for a volume written on the subject.

Within two months Doris was to become the third Mrs. Keiller, marrying him just before his forty-ninth birthday, and having signed a marriage contract renouncing the right to any claim, whilst accepting an allowance on the condition that she did not buy any furs or jewellery without her new husband's knowledge or consent. The wedding was announced to the staff at Avebury on November 14th and took place two days later at Caxton Hall in London. Telegrams were sent to the Mayfair Hotel. The honeymoon was to have been delayed until December 21st so that the newlyweds could spend Christmas in Paris, but at the last moment it was decided they should go immediately after the wedding. They returned to Avebury on December 1st.[205]

Doris Emerson Chapman was born in 1903, the daughter of Major-General Chapman of the Royal Marine Light Infantry. She was an artist, and had studied in Paris. She described her style as 'modernist', although she was equally accomplished as a traditional artist.[206]

Denis Grant King, who first met her when she returned to Avebury with Keiller following their honeymoon, describes her thus..

'Mrs Keiller is a fair tall woman, apparently about 30 but possibly more, with a Roman nose and a pleasant face. She has rather nice eyes with shyly drooping eyelids, which remind me of certain Eastern ladies whose long lashes were portrayed so seductively in an old edition of Burton's *Arabian Nights* familiar to me in my childhood. This impression contrasted somewhat oddly with her stubborn chin, and gave a hint of a character possessing conflicting traits, assurance, ambition, and shy reserve. She was dressed in a brown fur coat and black toque, and bore evidence of a discreet use of cosmetics. From what I hear she is now much more fashionable in her appearance than when she first came to Avebury to assist with the excavations. She seemed to be a trifle nervous on this occasion of her second arrival in Avebury, but was very affable...'.[207]

Denis Grant King, together with Young, was invited to the Manor on the day after Doris and Keiller's return for afternoon tea and a slice of iced wedding cake, whilst they listened politely to news of the latest fashions and fads in Paris.

Fig.50. Doris Emerson Chapman, the third Mrs Keiller
Alexander Keiller Museum, Avebury

Meals at the Manor were generally sumptuous affairs, whatever the time of day, although as a Scot, Keiller always preferred porridge for breakfast. Both luncheon and dinner began with wines and cocktails. Occasionally, selected members of the excavation and museum staff were invited to lunch, where they could expect a cold buffet, with meats carved by the under-butler, and a salad served with 'most embarrassingly attentive manner'. This was followed by an elaborate dessert, perhaps a fruit confectionery covered with whipped cream, and the meal concluded with cheese and biscuits.[208] To Keiller this was merely a functional and everyday occurrence, but to some of his guests it must have seemed like an extravagant banquet. Dinner parties were frequent, and often pre-dinner drinks went on until 11pm. Owing to this, the cook would not begin preparing the meal until 8pm, although according to his secretary Mrs Sorel-Taylour, the cook was caught out one night when Keiller requested dinner at 8pm prompt, and of course it was not ready!

He cared little for the cost of his meals, which must have been minuscule in proportion to his expenditure on the excavation work at Avebury. There was always the opportunity for a little luxury, and two examples that exist today can confirm this. In the museum at Avebury, often artefacts were packed away in whatever was to hand - a shining example being the wooden crate originally filled with port sent down by train from Fortnum & Masons in 1936.

Again, in the recent clearing of the pond site in the Manor grounds, it was discovered that the area had been used as a rubbish dump for the Manor during the 1930s. Endless discarded pottery jars of Gentleman's Relish, caviar, preserves (including of course Keiller marmalade), and other delicacies were unearthed.[209] Also brought to light however, was a considerable quantity of medicine bottles and apocathery cures, which either indicates that the inhabitants of the Manor were poorly a great deal of the time, or that too much rich food had its disadvantages!

42
CHANGE OF FORTUNES

BY THE CLOSE OF 1938, land purchases and excavation costs were beginning to take their toll on Keiller's marmalade fortune. Always willing to assist a fellow archaeologist financially in order to help their work, as demonstrated with Crawfords 'Antiquity' and the offer of paid leave to Leslie Grinsell's superior at Barclays, Keiller had in 1937 granted Trelawney Dayrell-Reed a 'Research Scholarship' to supplement his new position as Curator of the Pitt-Rivers Museum.[210]

When he wrote to Dayrell Reed in January 1939, Keiller said that he hoped to complete the work within the Circle at Avebury, 'but even this will not ... be possible without external subsidies'.[211]   To this end, he had considered withdrawing the allowance of £100 per annum, but changed his mind at the last moment, thus granting Dayrell-Reed a reprieve.

On February 1st, Keiller travelled to Exeter, taking the train with Doris, King, Norman Cook (Curator of the Avebury Museum), and Young. They stayed in the Rougemont Hotel, where Keiller insisted on pre-dinner cocktails of gin and vermouth for the entire party. The lecture was to be given to the Devon Archaeological & Exploration Society, a talk on 'Last Season's Excavations at Avebury'. Keiller spoke for seventy minutes with no written notes, his lecture accompanied by Kodachrome slides of the excavation. At the conclusion of his lecture, Keiller paid tribute to Gray, who was present, and the work that Gray had done in previous years at Avebury. King, who was unaware of Keiller's personal opinion of Gray, observed that Gray 'was visibly affected...and..he made a very good little speech which hardly concealed his surprise and gratification'.[212]

After packing up the slides and other equipment, the party returned to Avebury. Before the next season's excavations began, as though to put his seal of approval on King at last, Keiller sent him up to London to be measured up at Teague's in Jermyn Street, for an M.I.A.R. green blazer.[213]

By the Spring finances seemed to be back on an even keel, and the third season of excavation commenced on May 1st 1939, concentrating on the interior of the South East sector of the Circle. Preservation work and ditch clearing had continued throughout the winter months.

In this sector, Stukeley's records indicated the presence of a stone of great height, which he named the Obelisk, within a small circle. He described the Obelisk

Fig. 51. The Obelisk marker being set in place, 1939   *EH Photo Library*

as being at least six feet taller than the highest stone standing at present in Avebury. Of this smaller circle only two stones remained standing with a further three visible. Excavations revealed the original position of the Obelisk although the stone had been broken up and removed long before. The site of the Obelisk was marked by a large concrete grooved pillar which was designed by Keiller himself.

A curious pattern began to emerge when Keiller discovered a group of eight small sarsens. These seemed to be set in a rectangular sequence to the west of the Obelisk, within the southern circle. They were named Z-stones, and were duly re-erected in their stone holes. It was noted that this odd line of stones had been packed at the base with lumps of chalk of a type that could only have come from deep within the ditch of the henge, implying that the stone arrangement and ditch were constructed around the same time. A burning pit was also uncovered

Following his location of the 'Ringstone' through Stukeley's records in 1936, Keiller was able to confirm his findings by excavating, and uncovered the broken base of the Ringstone buried beneath the turf.

In early August the excavation was still under way, and Keiller wrote to Colonel Awdry to say that he had discovered two further buried stones in the space of an hour. This letter more than any revealed the extent of his commitment to Avebury...

'... If finances permit, this part of the monument ought to be one of the most astonishing, as well as impressive, in the whole of the Avebury complex. I will carry on for so long as I can, of course, even on the limited scale at present in operation here. But my financial situation, thanks to expenditure on the practical preservation of Avebury during the last few years will not continue for very much longer to be equal to the strain. I am selling my lands in Scotland which I inherited from my father, and which mean more to me than anything else in the world, and, if it is possible to continue work by so doing, Doris and I will in all probability move out of the Manor very shortly into some small house in the village. Even so I am afraid that independently I shall not be able to complete the work which I have regarded as a duty, and have undertaken as such. I hope at least to be able to finish the Southern Interior setting even if I cannot complete the South-East sector as I should like to do. Looking at the brighter side of the matter, however, the Circles of Avebury and the more important part of the West Kennet Avenue, is at least preserved for the nation for all time...'[214]

His words ring true in the present day, for when we walk around the stones of this World Heritage site we have a debt of gratitude to pay to this man who gave up so much for his dreams.

43
MAJOR IMPLICATIONS

EVENTS OF THE SUMMER were overshadowed by the threat of war. On July 16th, in his fiftieth year, Keiller signed up as a member of the Special Constabulary for the Marlborough Division, his number being 1301. He had the previous year written to Colonel Awdry asking his advice on what he should do *our Col..* *Awdry ?* when War became imminent, saying, '...I have served in the Navy, Army and Airforce. I was never a good pilot, and I should not make one now. I am rather hot with a machine gun; a 12 bore shotgun or a Luger pistol. I can lay out rectangular trenches with meticulous accuracy. ... Finally ... I have served a good many years, during the War and otherwise, in the "husher" branches of British Intelligence'.[214a]

One early August morning Avebury awoke to find '... with astonishment that the 9th Lancers, with 119 tanks and other vehicles, had entered the restored portion of West Kennet Avenue without [apparently] having requested permission to do so, and were actually parked there. The 10th Hussars were parked outside the South East Sector and in the village street ...'.[215] This had been organised through Keiller three weeks previously, but was a complete surprise to the rest of the village. Unfortunately, the soldiers parked some of their vehicles in the wrong area, having opened the gates which gave access to West Kennet Avenue and driven onto the field. On assurance that everything would be left as they found it, permission was granted (presumably by Keiller) for them to remain in this undesignated area for a few hours.

They did not keep to their word. When they left, the wheels and tracks of their vehicles cut up the turf, and the soldiers themselves left litter scattered across the whole area. Far worse, some of the stones in the West Kennet Avenue were defaced with graffiti by some of the reservists, provoking outrage from Keiller, and *no change here* *then* a heated campaign of correspondence with everyone from the CO of the Unit to the War Office.[216]

By August 26th, the outbreak of war seemed so imminent that matters were deemed serious enough to work overtime on the excavation site in order to reach a position where it could be closed down if necessary. It was on this busy day that Keiller's friend Commander Gould visited Avebury on his way to take up his duties under the Admiralty in Bath.

On September 3rd, War was declared on Germany following the invasion of Poland. The evacuation of mothers and children from London began that same day, and just after ten o'clock that evening over 70 children from the age of five upwards, together with five teachers, arrived in Avebury from a school at Customs

House in the East End of London. Twenty two of these children and one teacher were billeted temporarily at the Manor as had been arranged by Doris Keiller. An outbreak of Scarlet Fever shortly afterwards added to the upheaval.

Keiller himself was promoted to Inspector in the Special Constabulary and took up active duty in his role, as younger full time officers volunteered for the Armed Forces. King noted that 'he appears to appreciate certain points of totalitarian philosophy, but does not go the whole way'.[217]   During a visit to Avebury by J. B. Priestley, the author, shortly after the outbreak of war, Priestley told Keiller that he hoped the work in Avebury would not be interrupted 'by further Nazi annexations; though he agreed with Keiller that the Germans would be very thorough in archaeological enterprise. Nevertheless, they would expect the findings and conclusions to support the Aryan-race theory whatever happened'.[218]

'You know, deane, I never feel the parlour's so 'ome-like since Mr Keiller put up that stone'

Fig. 51a. Stuart Piggott's interpretation of local feeling
By kind permission of S. and A. Sanderson

44
FADING DREAMS

WITH LACK OF MANPOWER and resources, the excavations at Avebury ceased. During his long years in Avebury, Keiller had provided much work for local labourers and farm hands at a time when jobs were scarce, but the villagers regarded him with mixed feelings. His initial plans to move all buildings outside of the circle met with opposition from some quarters. There is no doubt that he removed several unsightly buildings, but the prospect of demolishing the remainder and relocating the village further afield proved to be understandably unpopular with local residents. Money for new houses was raised by public appeal, and it is worth noting that one contributor was Mr A. W. Lawrence, who donated the money in memory of his brother, Lawrence of Arabia.[219]

Even Keiller's excavations of the Circles had met with opposition from some village inhabitants who considered that the site should maintain its mystery and anonymity, by leaving the stones buried and the landscape untouched.

Much of Keiller's time after the outbreak of war was taken up with police work, and although the excavations continued on a limited basis, he spent most days on duty in the Marlborough area. He took his work seriously, studying for exams on various subjects such as Poison Gas. He later became known in his division and further afield as a fingerprints expert.

Shortly after his appointment as Inspector, Keiller was travelling with King in his car when they came upon a road accident, at which 'AK immediately assumed his new professional status with some inquisitorial dignity (in which, I suspect, he takes considerable pleasure), and I left him with note-book in hand taking particulars of the incident ...'.[220] His intense work pattern, often fifteen hours a day, would be occasionally broken by brief visits to London.

The 'hands', or rather what was left of the work gang from the excavations, were involved in various tasks around the village including the conversion of the old School into a public air raid shelter, and clearing the thistles and thorns from the Circle. They were also engaged in pulling up the cast iron railings around the graves and tombs in the village churchyard to be melted down and used for war munitions or aircraft. This campaign was yet another way of getting the public involved in the war effort, but in this instance, the majority of the scrap metal collected was totally unsuitable for these purposes.

Owing to the proximity of Yatesbury military camp, the Avebury area suffered *Really?* from many bombing raids. After one such raid in October 1940, Will Young and Denis Grant King, who were both at that time involved with the museum, went up to the East Kennet long barrow to see the damage done. When they arrived it was to find '... Police Inspector Keiller, who happened to be taking down official notes and measurements of the craters...'.[221]   The damage was not extensive.

On another occasion less than two weeks later, the Home Guard of which Young was a member, were presenting a 'Scattering and Dive Bombing Demonstration' for the public on the Marlborough Downs. Young recalls that there were approximately a thousand Home Guard and as many spectators. At 11.50 a.m, following a talk about gas, the highlight of the show was due -- a dive attack by

Fig. 52. Keiller in police uniform, Lafayette portrait   *P. Keiller*

104

Hurricane aircraft during which the Home Guard would carry out a practice in aiming. '...This item however, had to be cancelled at the last minute owing to their having a rather more important job in view. In short, a Nazi airman 'gate-crashed'. We were all looking up in anticipation of the final event, when the enemy plane dived out of the clouds and dropped two heavy HE bombs in the direction of Devil's Den, about a mile away from us. He was already being chased by the Hurricanes, and it was no doubt due to this fact that he missed his target. The bombs dropped into a ploughed field, and no damage was done. Thanks to the Nazi it made very good practice for us in scattering ... while at the same time it provided a much more exciting event to finish up the programme with than the one listed ..'.[222]

Fig. 53. Group photograph of the Regulars and Specials of the Marlborough Police Force (Keiller seated, centre), 1945 *Wiltshire Life Society* He looks really old for 56
Isn't this Doris?

Young also noted that following this impromptu entertainment the traffic was directed by the Special Police, under the supervision of Keiller, and everything went off without a hitch.

During the War years a convalescent home was created at nearby Yatesbury for soldiers and airmen injured during the course of duty. Keiller often used to call in at the home to ask if there were any Scottish men convalescing. Any fortunate Scots were then invited to the Manor at Avebury for afternoon tea. One young airman recalls Keiller's generous hospitality on many such afternoons, describing him as an excellent and entertaining host.[223]

Keiller was able to take an occasional break from his busy schedule to spend time on archaeological matters. In 1941 he was consulted along with Young on the routing of a new petrol pipe line near the Sanctuary, and he called in briefly on the first day of excavation to see how things were going, albeit for a brief visit, as more pressing matters were at hand.[224]

45
THE BEGINNING OF THE END

SINCE THE OUTBREAK OF WAR there had been an increasing estrangement between Keiller and Doris. Doris attributed it to her husband's neglect and infidelities, although the couple spent little time together between 1939 and 1941 owing to Keiller's police duties and Doris's work as a nurse in London. She was able to travel to Avebury on alternate weekends, but when Keiller visited London he preferred to take a suite at the Mayfair Hotel rather than stay with Doris.

Early in 1941, Doris began an affair which lasted for five months. When it was discovered, she ended it, hoping that she and Keiller might have some chance of a reconciliation, and it may have succeeded, for in September 1941, Keiller took her up to Morven on the train for her first visit to the Estate. His car had been sent up previously by rail, owing to the petrol rationing. The large house at Morven had been utilised earlier in the war as a home for evacuees from Glasgow, and also as a billet for army officers during training exercises in the surrounding countryside. The house did not fare well under this rigorous usage and lack of general care, and it must have been a shock for Keiller to see it in such a state of disrepair. It was on this visit that he decided to sell Avebury, and the lands at Morven, whilst retaining the house his father had built, 'Invercauld', to live in when the war was over.[225]

On returning from Scotland at the end of October, Keiller announced to his staff that the M.I.A.R. had ceased to exist. He declared that he was no longer able to carry on in Avebury due to financial worries, and in consequence of this the Museum would finally close at the end of November. He told Young, who was the only remaining member of the M.I.A.R. staff since Piggott had gone off to enlist, that he intended to offer the Monument and the Manor to the Nation. Keiller's announcement regarding the future of Avebury was nothing new. It had been rumoured in earlier months that he and Doris intended to leave Avebury for good.

Two weeks later Keiller left Avebury and did not return for some time. The Museum closed on November 30th, and the staff at the Manor left with several weeks wages owing. Despite frequent urgent messages in the preceding days from Young, there was no acknowledgement from Keiller, and it was left to Young to close things down at the Museum as he saw fit.[226]

Even before the outbreak of war, plans were underfoot to procure the purchase of Avebury for the Nation. In June 1939, Matheson of the National Trust wrote to the Office of Works expressing concern about Avebury.[227] F. J. E. Raby at the Office of Works replied, saying that it was likely, if changes occurred, that the monuments would come into their hands, although the Museum with its irreplaceable archives, was not scheduled. Raby did not think that Keiller would really want to run such risks with a unique site, but the position may not have been brought home to him in this light. Was there anyone, Raby wondered, possibly a good friend, who could make sure Keiller really understood this?

In fact, Keiller had made a proviso in his Will to ensure the safety of Avebury by the formation of the 'Morven Trust',[228] but this was unknown in official circles. By January 1943, negotiations were complete, and the National Trust were on the point of signing the contract for the purchase of Keiller's property in Avebury, excluding the Manor House, an area of some 950 acres, for £12,000. A Press Statement announced the purchase, and the Pilgrim Trust offered £10,000, with the remaining £2,000 given by I. D. Margery. This price represented the agricultural value of the property, and Keiller did not ask for any reimbursement of the large sum of money – in excess of £50,000 – that he had spent on excavation and preservation work. In modern terms £12,000 would be in the region of half a million pounds, suggesting that Keiller had spent in excess of two million on excavation and preservation.[229]

The War ended in May 1945, and everything began to settle tentatively into some semblance of normality. Keiller maintained his position with the Special Police, spending most of his time in Wiltshire, and in October was promoted to Superintendent. His rank and position were occasionally used to his advantage, as a young traffic policeman who pulled Keiller over recalls he was told in no uncertain terms that he was delaying a friend of the Chief Constable of Wiltshire, and sent away with a flea in his ear.[230]

In January 1945, on Keiller's suggestion, Young resumed his post as Curator of the Museum in Avebury. This time though, he was a representative of the Ministry of Works, who now maintained the site following the sale of land and acquisitions to the National Trust. Keiller, however, still kept a high profile, wandering in and out of the Museum at leisure with parties of friends, and quite often making most impossible demands on poor Young, who was no longer in his employ.

On January 17 1945, there was a fire in the large barn in the Manor farmyard that Keiller used as a garage. Not only did the fire destroy some of Keiller's cars, including the Citroen Kegresse and the Mercedes, but also boxes of finds (both archaeological and geological) from Morven, and Young spent much of those first few months retrieving what he could from the charred and water-damaged cases.

Attempts were made by the Ministry of Works to persuade Mrs Keiller to write a revised edition of *Is this your First Visit to Avebury?*,[231] the guide book she had written for sale at the Museum before the War. There were endless stumbling blocks, the path to reprinting hindered by Keiller's constant attention to detail, and the inclusion of photos and drawings from the original copy. By this time, Doris and Keiller were estranged once more. Since 1943 Doris had been living mostly in a cottage she had taken in London, which was initially intended as a home for both of them, but Keiller had not moved in with her.[231a]

In late August, Keiller was asked to resign from the Special Police, a request which made him particularly angry. The Special Police had a much reduced role following the end of the War, but Keiller was not eager to leave. He had always held an interest in Criminology, but perhaps the distinguished uniform was another reason for his reluctance to hand in his resignation. Following a meeting with the Deputy Chief Constable, it was agreed that he could stay on.

On the archaeological front, the war continued, albeit one-sided, with Maud Cunnington at Devizes. Young noted in his diary that '...It is a part of AK's childish manner that he cannot write a letter on any archaeological matter without making some caustic remark about Mrs Cunnington. It has become quite a mania with him, and since it's quite evident he is on the borderline of insanity in this respect, I object to his coupling my name with this strange obsession of his ...'.[232]

Although Young saw this feud as largely one-sided, and indeed considered it the reason why King was passed over for a position with the Wiltshire Archaeological Society, this was not necessarily the case. Until Keiller arrived in Wiltshire, the archaeology of the county had belonged largely to the Cunningtons. It is reasonable to assume that they did not take kindly to a stranger in their midst, albeit one with little or no archaeological background. Perhaps they did not go out of their way to make Keiller's presence welcome, and his grievances may have been justified.

46
PLEASANT DIVERSIONS

EARLY IN 1946, Keiller took up with a lady residing in the nearby village of Ogbourne St George,[233] one in a succession of mistresses. This affair with his 'Elizabeth' continued, and in February he gave two weeks notice to the tenants in one of his cottages in Manor Drive at Avebury, people who had lived there for many years, with the reason that it was needed for 'a friend'. The tenants moved into a parent's home, and after complete refurbishment, the new resident – 'Elizabeth' – moved in. Prior to the move, she had contacted the previous tenants, offering to pay for expenses, but she was told that they had not stooped so low as to accept assistance from the person who was the cause of them having to give up their home.[234]

Despite this apparent commitment to his 'Elizabeth', in July Keiller went to Scotland with his wife for a holiday, perhaps for one final attempt at a reconciliation, but more likely to confirm their domicile in Scotland. This holiday was cut short by a bout of rheumatics in his shoulder which warranted treatment in London. He did not return to Avebury again until January 15th 1947, when he resigned his post with the Special Police and handed in his uniform. He called to see Young at the Museum, declaring that he was returning to London and then taking a short holiday in St Moritz. Young noted that Keiller seemed distracted, and was not interested in talking about either archaeology or Avebury.

In May, Doris Keiller came to Avebury from London, staying only briefly before returning. The same day that she left, Keiller arrived at the Manor directly from Scotland. This cat and mouse game continued, until it came to a head in July. Doris became worried about Keiller's absence and that of his driver, after hearing nothing of him for two weeks. She knew that Keiller had become friendly with Gabrielle Styles, an international golfer and cattle ranch heiress, but was completely stunned to learn that they had run away to France together. Keiller wrote to Doris, asking her to release him 'either by separation or divorce'. The marriage was over. Even Young, who was not a fan of the third Mrs Keiller, was shocked by Keiller's apparent lack of feeling, when Doris showed him the letter and 'broke down and wept as though her heart would break'.[235]

As if to take her mind off personal matters, Doris decided to put her efforts into producing a reliable yet popular book on the monument of Avebury, and also Windmill Hill, although she did not begin work on this book until 1948. By now she had successfully completed the second edition of the Museum guide book. An

109

arrangement was made so that Doris's visits to the Manor would not clash with those of Keiller and Mrs Styles, in accordance with their 'mutual agreement regarding their present relations'.[236]

At first Keiller was quite agreeable for her to go ahead with her book, telling her that she could make use of the Manor library and any of the unpublished material in the Museum Archives. However by August he had changed his mind.

Following a weekend visit to the Manor, Keiller asked Young, who was Custodian at the Museum, for the key of the deed box in the Archives. He took some items from the box and then locked it, taking the key back to London. This, he told Young, was to prevent Mrs Keiller from getting at any of his excavation notes. He had also locked up the Drawing Office in the Manor for the same reason. Despite these obstacles, Doris continued work on her book, enlisting the help of Stuart Piggott at one stage. The work was never published.

In 1949 Keiller was horrified to discover that during the Blitz, the 'Tally-Ho Warehouse' in London had been bombed, and the remains of what he had in storage there had been shovelled into 105 sacks. These contained all manner of items, including Egyptian urns and a vast collection of arrowheads from places as diverse as North and South America, and Ireland. Keiller sent all of these sacks to Young at Avebury, requesting that he did whatever he could with them. As Keiller had been, Young was heartbroken to find the collections virtually destroyed, the glass display cases shattered and lying amongst the broken artefacts. He salvaged what he could, and repaired many of the broken arrowheads.[237]

Not one to sit back and let life go by, Keiller was in the headlines in March of 1950 under the unlikely heading 'Jam Man to pay £5,000'.[238] This followed his agreement to pay this sum in costs to a divorce court owing to 'allegations of misconduct with Mrs Gabrielle M. Styles', whose husband had filed for a divorce. Both Keiller and the Styles had a flat at 'Fairacres' on the outskirts of London, a crescent shaped modern apartment block which looked out on to Roehampton golf course, and it was at 'Fairacres' the adultery was alleged to have taken place. As a couple they had been together for almost three years by this time, and the court case was something of a technicality. Doris, however, would not grant Keiller a divorce, and so the couple were, for the present, not able to marry.

After the court case, Keiller and Mrs Styles visited Ireland, touring several notable museums there, and perhaps visiting Glenveagh Castle in Co Donegal where Gabrielle had spent many happy childhood summers.[239] When they returned to England, they took up residence once more in London.

Fig. 54. Gabrielle Styles   *Giles Currie*

47
GABRIELLE

GABRIELLE MURIEL RITCHIE was born August 10th, 1908 in North Berwick, Scotland, where her parents were taking a golfing holiday. She was educated privately, and took up golf at an early age.

By 1939, having been married twice with a young son from her first marriage, her golfing career was flourishing, and she was winning tournaments both here and abroad. The War put a temporary halt to this, and she took to driving of a different sort when she joined the L.C.C. Auxiliary Ambulance Service, working in a heavily bombed area of London.

111

After the War she continued golfing, and in 1948 won the Ladies Open Championship in Switzerland, Luxembourg and Monaco, as well as becoming a member of the England team in Home Internationals. When she met Keiller, who himself had an interest in the sport and made an ideal partner, she was at the height of her career.[240]

Fig. 55. Keiller in the early 1950s   *WA&NHS Library, Devizes*

48
SUNRISE AT MORVEN

KEILLER'S HEALTH began to deteriorate. He spent the first three months of 1951 in the South of France, and then returned to London for an operation on his throat. Having finally persuaded Doris to give him a divorce, he married Gabrielle the day after it came through in late Spring that year. Young sent a letter to Keiller, saying, 'I am so glad that you are now free to marry the one who has looked after you with so much devotion the past four years; one whose happiness is so clearly wrapped up with yours for good'.[241]

In 1953, they moved to Telegraph Cottage in Kingston Hill, Surrey. The house had been a wartime residence for General Eisenhower, and had once been on the semaphore route from Portsmouth to the Admiralty. Here they made their home together. Gabrielle created an idyllic woodland garden from the four and a half acre wilderness, an impressive setting for contemporary sculptures which were to become, after Keiller's death, a part of her vast surrealist art collection. This new home was nestled between two golf courses, one of which could be reached via a gate in the garden, thus allowing Gabrielle and Keiller to indulge this shared pastime. Often Keiller would film her practising her strokes on his cinecamera, so that later she could watch her play and improve upon her weaknesses.

In March 1955, almost 13 years after Keiller had first offered Avebury Manor to the nation, he found a buyer, the botanist Sir Frances Knowles. Contracts were signed on March 10th, and Young, who was still then Custodian of the Museum, wrote to Keiller saying that he had looked up the quotation for that date in the Christopher Robin Birthday Book.[242] During the West Kennet and Avebury excavations, Young and Keiller had each year looked up the quotations for the first day of digging, taking them as 'omens'.

On moving from the Manor, Keiller gave two of his books to Young but the remainder were taken back to Surrey. Many of the excavation records and surveys were however left in the Manor, and only retrieved by Young almost a year later. The Dovecote was filled with finds from two decades of excavations, and it was only much later that these were finally moved.

Keiller's health continued to deteriorate, and by September 1955 the specialists were able to diagnose his condition as terminal cancer. The operation on his throat four years previously had not prevented the spread of malignant cells to his lung, but this was not discovered until it was too late for treatment to be of any benefit. All that could be done was to make his last days as comfortable as possible.

113

He made a final will, leaving everything to Gabrielle but also making provisos should her death closely follow his own. One of these provisos would have been the formation of the Keiller Anti-Cancer Trust, selling off all of his estate to form such a Trust, the monies to be invested and used for the purpose of attacking and allaying the disease of cancer.[243]

On October 29th 1955 Alexander Keiller died at home in Kingston Hill, Surrey. He was cremated, and his ashes buried in the walls of Gairn Castle which he had reserved for this purpose when he sold the rest of his estate in Morven. He had said of Gairn that some of his earliest memories of the castle in his life consisted of crawling about on its dilapidated walls.[244] Even today, the ruins (actually a fortified hunting lodge rather than a castle), protected on three sides by towering pines, look across to the heather-clad slopes of the Scottish Highlands. At the very end he came to rest in the place that he had always called home.

Fig. 56. Keiller's final resting place at Morven   *Author*

His obituary in *The Times* centred mainly on his work at Avebury, concluding that here prehistoric man had put forth one of his mightiest efforts, and after centuries of decay the site had been preserved for future generations.[245]

Tributes poured in from fellow archaeologists such as Gray, Piggott, and Christopher Hawkes. Professor Hawkes had once said ' we are well aware how large is our debt to him [Keiller] for his scrupulously careful excavations are, quite apart from the great interest of the results, to be ranked as a permanent credit to British

Archaeology'.[246]

Denis Grant King wrote of him later, 'The spirit of friendship and mutual aid which gathered people together to work for the excavation and restoration of the Avebury monument was in many ways quite unique. It was not only a great pioneer work in archaeology, but it was also a gallant and genuine attempt to deal with the greater problems of human relationships which has disturbed mankind almost from the time and genesis of human society'.[247]

Gabrielle immediately gave up golf, and some time later turned to the Roman Catholic faith. She worked for over a decade at the British Museum as a volunteer, and also took up photography, another interest of her late husband's. In the years following his death, she commissioned Dr Smith to write up a report on the Windmill Hill and Avebury excavations. This was published in 1965 with an introduction written by Stuart Piggott.

Keiller's Sizaire-Berwick, which he had owned for over forty years, was restored and presented to the National Motor Museum at Beaulieu. In 1966, the museum at Avebury and the collection housed there was given to the nation by Deed of Gift, passing into the care of English Heritage at its formation in 1984. The museum has been managed by the National Trust – which owns the building – since 1994. It is rumoured that somewhere in Avebury a disused well is filled with items cleared out from the Museum archives at Avebury after his death, including a pair of old skis.

Above all, Keiller would like to have been remembered as an archaeologist. He had described the subject as 'an insidious vice', of which once one became an addict it was exceedingly difficult to break oneself free.[248]

It has been said that 'men built temples not out of fear but because they believed that by creating something that outlived them they also survived, immortal, blessed with divinity no scepticism could mute'.[249] This observation could have been true for the prehistoric builders of Avebury, but is echoed in the present through Keiller's excavation and preservation of the site. What we see today is largely due to his efforts, and through his achievement he still lives on.

NOTES AND REFERENCES

List of Abbreviations

AKM - Alexander Keiller Museum All quotes by kind permission of the Alexander Keiller Museum and English Heritage

DGK - Dennis Grant King (All quotes by kind permission of Margaret Nurse, copyright holder)

NMM - National Motor Museum, Beaulieu

PRO - Public Record Office, London.(Crown Copyright material in the PRO is reproduced by permission of the Controller of Her Majesty's Stationery Office)

RCAHM - Royal Commission for Ancient & Historic Monuments (All quotes from NMR, Swindon by kind permission, Crown Copyright: RCAHM)

RCAHMS - Royal Commission for Ancient & Historic Monuments Scotland (All quotes from the Alexander Keiller Collection in NMR Scotland, Crown Copyright: RCAHMS)

SCGB - Ski Club of Great Britain

SRO - Scottish Record Office (All quotes by kind permission of the Keeper of Records of Scotland)

WA&NHS - Wiltshire Archaeological & Natural History Society (All quotes by kind permission of the WA&NHS Library)

All quotes from Professor Piggott appear by kind permission of Stewart and Alison Sanderson, literary executors.

1 Ian Keiller pers comm.

2 Dundee Library Archive & Patricia Keiller (New Zealand).

3 Mathew, W M. John Mitchell Keiller. Forthcoming. New Dictionary of National Biography.

4 Mathew, W M. John Mitchell Keiller. Forthcoming. New Dictionary of National Biography.

5 Mathew, W M. John Mitchell Keiller.John Mitchell Keiller. Forthcoming. New Dictionary of National Biography.

6 AKM, correspondence Keiller to Norris 23 January 1938.

7 Stakis Balmoral, Ballater. The Story of the Craigendarroch. 1991.

8 Stakis Balmoral, Ballater. The Story of the Craigendarroch. 1991.

9 Mathew, W M. John Mitchell Keiller. 1998. New Dictionary of National Biography.

10 Mathew, W M. John Mitchell Keiller. 1998. New Dictionary of National Biography.

11 Dundee Library Archive. Dundee Advertiser 11 May 1900.

12 Hazelwood Preparatory School. The Nutshell. 1903.

13 Eton College Register.

14 Recumbent Stone Circles. The Recumbent type of stone circle is predominant in North East Scotland, and its name derives from the stone that lies always at the South West point of the circle where it is flanked by two uprights. Quite often the recumbent is of a different stone to the rest of the circle. It is thought that these circles had a lunar alignment, and were linked closely with death and ritual. It is not unusual to have a burial site such as a cairn, barrow or cist inside the circle.

15 Simpson was appointed librarian to Aberdeen University in 1926 following a period as a Lecturer in History. His knowledge of all matters archaeological was extensive, but his specialist area was castles, about which he wrote several books following years of excavation work. Information from Leslie Ferguson, RCAHMS.

16 Mathew, W M. Minutes from 'James Keiller & Sons Ltd' Board Meetings 1910-1918.

17 SCGB Ski Notes & Queries Vol III 1926-28, 210.

17a AKM, correspondence Keiller to Awdry 26

Sept 1938.

18 SRO/CS46 no. 12 of August 1919.

19 National Portrait Gallery Archive.

20 NMM Archive.

21 NMM Archive.

22 NMM Archive.

23 Michael Ware, NMM. Article from Dundee Courier & Advertiser 2 July 1988.

24 Royal Air Force PMC, Innsworth.

24a Charles Rumney Samson was the first man to make a take-off from a ship in an aircraft in January 1912. His squadron went out to France early in the Great War to defend England from the Zeppelin threat, and the vehicles he took out with him were some of the first to be fitted with armour protection, the armour being designed by his brother Felix, who was also a member of the squadron – the first car being known as the 'Iron Duke'.

25 David Fletcher, Tank Museum, Bovington.

25a NMM Archive, from L'Histoire Phenomenale - Sizaire Freres, interview with Maurice Sizaire.

26 NMM Archive.

26a AKM, correspondence Keiller to Awdry 26 Sept 1938.

27 Royal Air Force PMC, Innsworth.

27a AKM, correspondence Keiller to Raby 6 Aug 1936.

28 Moira Gittos, Fleet Air Arm Museum.

29 Royal Air Force PMC, Innsworth.

30 SCGB Ski Notes & Queries Vol III 1926-28, 210.

31 Erskine Childers was a larger than life character, in contrast an ex-Boer war trooper, Clerk to the House of Commons, official historian, gun-runner, novelist, and romantic idealist. He was shot by the Irish as a traitor in 1922.

32 AKM, DGK Diaries, 75.

33 Mathew, W. M. Minutes from 'James Keiller & Sons Ltd' Board Meetings 1910-1918.

34 SRO/CS46 no. 12 of August 1919. It is feasible, as with later wives, that Florence signed a pre-nuptial agreement.

35 Cornish Record Office, with kind assistance of M Wright & T O'Hanlon.

36 WA&NHS Library, 1923 Catalogue of Charles Street Library.

37 Keiller 1922.

38 Murray 1921.

39 AKM, correspondence Keiller to Rose 23 October 1930.

40 Michael Pitts & Hilary Howard, Interview with P D Sorel Taylour 1979.

41 Crawford, OGS, 1955, 166.

42 Crawford, OGS The Sunday Observer 8 July 1923.

43 AKM, correspondence Crawford to Keiller 19 May 1930.

44 AKM, correspondence Keiller to Editor The Scotsman 15 September 1923.

45 AKM, correspondence Keiller to Crawford 14 September 1923.

46 AKM, correspondence Keiller to Crawford 21 August 1923.

47 AKM, correspondence Keiller to Crawford 14 September 1923.

48 Hampshire County Library Archive, Basingstoke.

49 SRO, CS/285/1935/181.

50 AKM, correspondence Keiller to Crawford 5 April 1924.

51 AKM, correspondence Keiller to Crawford 7 April 1924.

52 AKM, correspondence Keiller to Kendall 9 July 1924.

53 Quoted in The Times on 5 December 1924 from a speech made by Crawford to the Society of Antiquaries.

54 AKM, review from Dundee Courier & Advertiser August 1928.

55 AKM, correspondence Keiller to Kendall 26 August 1924.

56 AKM, correspondence Keiller to Kendall 25 October 1924.

57 AKM, correspondence Keiller to Newcombe at Wallace Heaton, 16 June 1936.

58 AKM, correspondence Keiller to Wallace Heaton, 19 March 1934.

59 Author's interview with Stuart Piggott, 1991.

60 Wood, J 1974 August edition. 1924 Hispano-Suiza.Classic Car Magazine.

61 NMM.

62 Cunnington 1975, 109.

63 Cunnington 1975, ix.

64 Cunnington 1975, ix.

65 Malone 1989, 65. 66 AKM, correspondence

Keiller to Crawford 31 May 1927.

65a Young had been engaged by the Cunningtons for their work at the Sanctuary, Avebury and Woodhenge (a structure close to Stonehenge, similar to the Sanctuary) before he was first introduced to Keiller at Windmill Hill by Gray . Keiller later appointed him Curator of the Museum at Avebury, where he remained (either side of the War) until his retirement in 1965.

67 AKM, The Times 5 February 1932.

68 Dr William Stukeley was an 18th century antiquarian who made extensive study of Avebury and other prehistoric sites. It is entirely due to Stukeley and other antiquaries such as Aubrey that we have early records of stone circles and monuments before later destruction of the sites took place. During Stukeley's time, almost the whole of the Sanctuary near Avebury was destroyed in one year, and many stones within the Henge and the Avenue were also broken up.

69 Ucko et al ,1991, 246.

70 RCAHMS. ABD/538

71 Steer 1996, McGregor.

72 AKM, correspondence Keiller to Childe 31 August 1932

72a Keiller, 1927, 2,4,7,8. 1928, 19.

73 RCAHMS 1979/24 MS/106/29.

74 AKM, correspondence Keiller to Gray 10 April 1926.

75 Source:National Monuments Record, Swindon. Copyright held by Giles Currie.

76 AKM, correspondence Keiller to Crawford.

77 AKM, Cinefilm. Letter reference 5 May 1925.

78 Davis 1981.

79 Dundee Library Archive, by kind permission.

80 From John Reynolds, Citroen Car Club. November 1923. Estate Work by Motorcar. The Motor, 8/29.

81 Crawford 1955,182

82 AKM, correspondence Crawford to Keiller 10 March 1928.

83 Crawford 1955,182.

84 PRO Work 14/498 Stonehenge correspondence Keiller to Office of Works 24 September 1928.

85 PRO Work 14/498 Stonehenge correspondence Keiller to Office of Works

22 September 1928.

86 PRO Work 14/498 Stonehenge correspondence Crawford to Bushe Fox 18 April 1929.

87 PRO Work 14/498 Stonehenge correspondence Keiller to Office of Works 20 September 1928.

88 AKM, correspondence Keiller to Gray 27 March 1928.

89 AKM, correspondence Keiller to Gray 28 April 1928.

90 AKM, correspondence Keiller to Gray 4 May 1928.

91 AKM, correspondence Keiller to Kendall 13 July 1926.

92 AKM, correspondence Clay to Keiller 3 May 1928.

93 AKM, correspondence Peers to Keiller 12 June 1928.

94 RCAHMS Manuscript extract MS/106/30

95 AKM, correspondence Keiller to Childe 11 December 1928.

96 AKM, correspondence Keiller to Gray 18 March 1929.

97 AKM, correspondence Keiller to Piggott 26 May 1929.

98 AKM, correspondence Keiller to Crawford 13 Dec 1926.

99 Antiquity 57, 1983, 28-37.

100 Antiquity 57, 1983, 28-37.

101 AKM, correspondence Keiller to Gray 1 October 1929.

102 AKM, correspondence Keiller to Crawford 1 March 1926.

103 Michael Brisby, from Conway 1983, 72.

104 Most of the information regarding Keiller's Bugattis was kindly provided by The Bugatti Trust.

105 Mortimer 1991,57.

106 Author interview with Anne Keiller Greig, March 1996.

107 AKM, correspondence Keiller to Gray 1 October 1929.

108 SRO, CS/258/181/2.

109 AKM, correspondence Keiller to Hogarth 28 July 1930.

110 AKM, correspondence Keiller to Norrington 10 August 1931.

111 Miss Marjorie James was Keiller's

archaeological assistant from around 1931, when she helped with the Windmill Hill Reports. She left his employment in 1938 to get married.

112 AKM, correspondence Keiller to Norrington 10 August 1931.

113 WA&NHS Library, Young Diaries.

114 WA&NHS Library, Young Diaries.

115 Captain James Stuart Hamilton Moore B A, O B E. Keiller first met Moore in 1917, when Moore was Chief Prisoner Interrogator for the British Intelligence Service. After the War he was offered a position in a firm in which Keiller was Director. In later years Keiller suggested Moore as a translator for Clarendon Press owing to his 'remarkable knowledge of German' (AKM,5 March 1926).

116 AKM, correspondence Keiller to Norrington, 20 September 1930.

117 Antiquity 57, 1983, 28-37.

118 AKM, correspondence Keiller to Green, 3 December 1936.

119 SCGB 1926-28 Ski Notes & Queries Vol III, 210.

120 SCGB Yearbook 1956, 110.

121 Wallace Heaton was founder of a specialist photographic company in London. Although the company is now well known internationally, in Keiller's day it was still small enough to grant a personal reply by Wallace Heaton himself to some of Keiller's correspondence.

122 AKM, correspondence Keiller to Wallace Heaton 1924.

123 AKM, correspondence Keiller to Norrington 23 January 1932.

124 AKM, correspondence Keiller to Norrington 23 January 1932.

125 AKM, correspondence Keiller to Norrington 5 March 1932.

126 Author's interview with Piggott, 1991.

127 SCGB Yearbook 1956, 110.

128 Kay Duncan did not return to work for Keiller. She was married later in the 1930s to Bindon Blood, a direct descendant of the Colonel Blood who stole the Crown Jewels, and they retired to live in Majorca.

129 AKM The Times 5 August 1932.

130 AKM The Times 5 August 1932.

131 Leslie Valentine Grinsell is best known for his many published works on Bronze Age Barrows. + Lederhosen

132 AKM The Times 5 August 1932.

132a Pub. The Archaeological Journal Vol LXXXVIII,1932, 67.

133 Author's interview with Piggott, 1991.

134 AKM, correspondence Piggott to Keiller 9 October 1934.

135 AKM, correspondence Keiller to Passmore 16 May 1933.

136 WA&NHS Library, Young Diaries 1 April 1933.

137 Correspondence Grinsell to author 16 April 1992.

138 AKM, correspondence Keiller to Norrington 9 August 1933.

139 Antiquity 57, 1983, 28-37.

140 AKM, correspondence Keiller to Dayrell-Reed 23 November 1933.

140a AKM, correspondence Keiller to Dayrell-Reed 23 November 1933.

141 Hawkes,J 1982 Mortimer Wheeler - Adventurer in Archaeology (London).

141a AKM, correspondence Keiller 12 April 1937

141b SRO, CS/258/181/2.

142 Author's interview with Piggott, 1991.

143 Constable Publishers. Chitty 1991, 26.

144 Jonathan Betts, who is currently researching the life of Rupert Gould for a forthcoming biography.

145 Stukeley's Manuscripts were bought by Keiller in 1924 on the sale of family papers. They now reside at the Bodleian Library in Oxford. Reference in AKM, correspondence Keiller to Cunnington 30 May 1930.

146 Smith, 1966, 180.

147 AKM, DGK Diaries.

148 Beakers first appeared in Britain from the continent around 2600 BC. The name 'Beaker' originates from the distinctive pots they made which were often buried with their dead beneath round barrows.

149 AKM, correspondence Keiller to Passmore 4 September 1934.

150 Keiller designed the concrete stelae himself in his office at Avebury Manor, ensuring that the finished result looked as unlike the sarsen

stones as possible, so that the two would not be confused.

151 In 1912, Maud Cunnington had re-erected one of the West Kennet Avenue stones, unfortunately the wrong way up. In July 1935, Keiller wrote to Passmore, 'At the moment we are in process of taking down stone 10 (Mrs Cunnington's unfortunate effort), and re-erecting it in its correct position, and, for a change, with its base in the ground instead of the air'.

152 Constable Publishers. Chitty 1991,62.

153 Barbara Laidler assisted with the excavations at West Kennet Avenue. Although described by Piggott as an 'entertainer', she did have a report published with Young in the Wiltshire Archaeological Magazine June 1938, entitled A Surface Flint Industry from a site near Stonehenge. Keiller's nickname for her was 'Little One'.

154 Prof. C.Thurstan Shaw is a well known archaeologist and anthropologist who has had a long and varied academic career, having much work published in both fields on Nigeria. See Who's Who1996. whe's ? Thurstan? yes

155 SRO, CS/258/181/2.

156 WA&NHS Library, Young Diaries January 1964.

157 Antiquity 57, 1983, 28-37.

158 Constable Publishers.Chitty 1991, 62.

159 AKM, correspondence Keiller to Passmore 8 April 1935.

160 AKM, correspondence Keiller to Norrington 27 March 1935.

161 Author's interview with Piggott, 1991.

162 Constable Publishers.Chitty 1991,62.

163 Chapman & Keiller 1936, Antiquity X, 207-209.

164 Constable pub.,Chitty, 1991,336.

164a Chatto & Windus pub., Hopkinson, L P, 1988,101.

164b Private Source.

165 AKM, correspondence Keiller to Piggott 9 October 1934.

166 Copy of this album at WA&NHS Library, Devizes.

167 AKM, correspondence Keiller to Ormsby-Gore 21 March 1937.

Keiller's interest in boxing spanned many years, and he had helped to found the Basingstoke Amateur Boxing Club probably in the 1920's when he was married to Veronica, who lived nearby. Often he would take parties from Avebury, including Young and Doris Chapman, to see fights at local venues. He much preferred amateur fights, and often donated prize money towards such competitions, including the 'Stable Lads Boxing Competition' held at Marlborough in 1939.

168 AKM, correspondence Keiller to Clark 11 March 1936.

169 AKM, correspondence Keiller to Green 29 November 1936.

170 AKM, correspondence Keiller to Green 3 December 1936.

171Antiquity 57, 1983, 28-37.

172 WA&NHS Library, Young Diaries.

173 AKM, correspondence Keiller to Passmore 18 July 1936.

174 Keiller,A & Piggott,S, 1939,133-49.

175 Antiquity, Vol XIII No 50, June 1939, 223.

176 AKM, correspondence Keiller to Cook 22 June 1937

177 First Report of the Sub-Committee of South-Western Group of Museums and Art Galleries on the Petrological Identification of Stone Axes, PPS,vii (1941), 50-72.

178 Keiller & Piggott, 1938.

179 AKM, correspondence Keiller to Piggott 1 November 1935.

180 AKM, correspondence Keiller to Norrington 3 December 1936.

181 AKM, correspondence Keiller to Norris 23 January 1938.

182 AKM, correspondence Keiller to Kendrick 19 July 1936.

183 WA&NHS Library, Young Diaries.

184 AKM, correspondence Keiller to Norrington 9 June 1937.

185 L V Grinsell pers comm 16 April 1992.

186 AKM, correspondence Keiller to Awdry 27 August 1937.

187 Authors interview with Winifred Jarman 14 October 1991.

188 AKM, DGK Diaries.

189 Authors interview with Mrs Ovens (nee Perry) 1992.

190 Author's interview with Piggott, 1991.

191 Author's interview with Piggott, 1991.

192 AKM, Ros Cleal interview with Elizabeth Lillie (nee Neal) 4 March 1995.

193 AKM, DGK Diaries, 57.

193a AKM, correspondence Keiller to Norris, 31 Jan 1938.

194 AKM, correspondence Keiller to Ormsby-Gore 21 March 1937.

195 AKM, correspondence Keiller to Ormsby-Gore 26 January 1937.

196 AKM, correspondence Keiller to Awdry 10 August 1939.

197 AKM, correspondence Keiller to Cook 6 April 1937.

198 Author's interview with Piggott, 1991.

199 AKM, 6 July 1938 The Times.

200 Authors interview with Ian McPhail, who convalesced at nearby Yatesbury, and was one of Keiller's privileged Scottish guests. 1994.

201 AKM, DGK Diaries, 27.

202 AKM, correspondence Keiller to Kendrick 29 June 1938.

203 AKM, correspondence Keiller to Kendrick 29 June 1938.

204 AKM, correspondence Keiller to Norrington 12 September 1938.

205 AKM, DGK Diaries, 85.

206 AKM, DGK Diaries, 256.

207 AKM, DGK Diaries, 85.

208 AKM, DGK Diaries, 81.

209 Chris Gingell, National Trust. AKM Recent Archive.

210 Holroyd, 1975, 19. Dayrell-Reed was an archaeologist, poet and anti-aircraft pioneer. He was the author of two archaeological works ('The First Battle of Britain' and 'The Rise of Wessex') which were uniquely interspersed with pages of his poetry. He kept a farm in Dorset, from where he tried to shoot down with his double barrelled shotgun a plane which was disturbing his afternoon rest. He was arrested for attempted murder, but found not guilty. Described as a black bearded fanatic, he was noted for the violence of his Oxford stammer, and loud dress which consisted of check tweeds, and revolutionary red socks. Living on a farm in deepest Dorset, he considered himself a 'country homosexual'.

211 AKM, correspondence Keiller to Dayrell-Reed 29 January 1939.

212 AKM, DGK Diaries, 131.

213 AKM, DGK Diaries, 229.

214 AKM, correspondence Keiller to Awdry 10 August 1939.

214a AKM, correspondence Keiller to Awdry 26 September 1938.

215 WA&NHS Library, Young Diaries, August 1939.

216 AKM, DGK Diaries, 74-80, also correspondence 15 August 1939.

217 AKM, DGK Diaries, 99.

218 AKM, DGK Diaries, 207.

219 PRO, London. Work/14 Avebury.

220 AKM, DGK Diaries, 115.

221 WA&NHS Library, Young Diaries, October 1940.

222 WA&NHS Library, Young Diaries, November 1940.

223 Authors interview with Ian McPhail 1994.

224 WA&NHS Library, Young Diaries, 20 June 1941.

225 AKM, Doris Keiller Collection

226 WA&NHS Library, Young Diaries, 30 November 1941. Owing to demand the museum was later reopened.

227 PRO, London. Work/14 Avebury.

228 PRO, London. Work/14 Avebury.

229 PRO, London. Work/14 Avebury. Statistics suggested by London School of Economics, UOL.

230 David Davidge, story related to him by Frank Dummett, retired Wiltshire policeman.

231 Chapman, 1939.

231a AKM, Doris Keiller Collection.

232 WA&NHS Library, Young Diaries, 2 November 1945.

233 WA&NHS Library, Young Diaries, February 1946.

234 WA&NHS Library, Young Diaries, 18 March 1946.

235 WA&NHS Library, Young Diaries, 21 July 1948.

236 WA&NHS Library, Young Diaries, 23 August 1948.

237 WA&NHS Library, Young Diaries, January 1949.

238 WA&NHS Library, Young Diaries, 21 March 1950 from The Daily Graphic.
239 Obituary January 10 1996 The Times.
240 Obituary January 10 1996 The Times.
241 AKM, correspondence Young to Keiller, April 1951.
242 WA&NHS Library, Young Diaries - This book remained for a time at the museum, and had been a gift from Antonia White in the 1930s.
243 Somerset House, Keiller 1956.

244 AKM, correspondence Keiller to Piggott 25 April 1932.
245 Obituary November 1955 The Times.
246 Hawkes & Kendrick, 1932, 58.
247 WA&NHS Library, letter from DGK accompanying remaining Young Diaries that were bequeathed to the Library by King.
248 AKM, correspondence Keiller to Wilkinson 14 June 1936.
249 Burnett 1982.

CARS

1913 'Prince Henry' Austro Daimler, sports model, only two hundred made. No other details.

1914 Sizaire-Berwick Reg. SB 785. Owned from new until his death in 1955. Now owned by the National Trust.

1923 Citroën Kegresse. Reg. SA 6623. Used until 1939 Destroyed in Manor Garage fire 1945(Young Diaries).

1924 Bugatti. No details. Possible crash victim.

1925 Hispano Suiza, Reg. XX 3883. Behring Auto Museum, USA.

1926 Bugatti Type 35. Reg. YM 9558. 8-cyl. 2 litre Went to Esson-Scott in 1930.

1927 Bugatti Type 35 TC Reg. NAE 194. Chassis No. 4849. 2.3 litre. Was until 1983 in the Harrah collection in Reno, Nevada, USA, but the collection has since been dispersed. Original price £630.

1920's (late) Mercedes. Destroyed by fire in Manor garage 1945 (Young Diaries) .

1930 MG Midget. (maybe the 18/80 2.5l 6 cyl, but most likely the Midget). No other details.

1948 Triumph two-seater touring car. Possibly Triumph Roadster, in production from 1946-49. Not many 1948 models survive. No other details.(Same model of car as was used by Bergerac in the TV series of the same name)

With regard to motoring research, I am indebted to Michael Brisby who set me on my way with all of Keillers cars, to Julie P Bate at the Bugatti Trust, Uwe Hucke (Bugatti), David Fletcher of the Tank Museum (Sizaire-Berwick), Malcolm Jeal, Michael Ware of the National Motor Museum, Peter Hull of the Michael Sedgwick Memorial Trust, who put me right on some of the more technical facts of my motoring sections; Brooklands Museum, and the following car clubs and their members, who were only too pleased to supply me with information to the best of their ability: MG Octagon Club; Triumph Roadster Club; Club Triumph; Citroen Car Club; Traction Owners Club.

*Keiller was not in any way involved with the motor company 'Grice Wood Keiller' (GWK), founded in 1910, although a distant cousin of his, C M Keiller, was the "K" of the company. It is interesting that for a time, production of this car was at the Cordwallis Works in Maidenhead, known locally as the Jam Factory and erstwhile home of 'St Martins Chunky Marmalade'.

SOCIETIES, COMMITTEES AND CLUBS

Fellow of the Society of Antiquaries from 1927

Fellow of the Geological Society from 1928

Fellow of the Society of Antiquaries (Scotland)

Life member Somerset Archaeological Society

Life member Wiltshire Archaeological Society

Corresponding member German Archaeological Institute 1934

British Organising Committee for the First International Congress of Prehistoric and Protohistoric Sciences 1932

Chairman Sub-Committee for the Petrological Identification of Stone Implements (South Western Group of Museums and Art Galleries)1936.

President British Ski Jumping Club 1932

Ski Club of Great Britain -Hon Sec & Treasurer of SCGB before its amalgamation with British Ski Association.

Ski Club Alpina

Schweizerische Akademische Ski Club

Hon. Mem. Kandahar Ski Club of Muerren

Hon. Mem. Maloja Ski Club

Brooklands Automobile Racing Club 1913-1938

EXCAVATIONS AND SURVEYS IN ENGLAND
(reproduced by kind permission of NMR, Swindon)

1925-27
WINDMILL HILL, WILTSHIRE
Classification:Neolithic Causewayed enclosure
Auspice:Private
Funding:Private
Directors:Alexander Keiller & Harold St George Gray
Finds Holder: AKM / Devizes Museum
Archive: AKM / Devizes Museum / NMRC, Swindon (RCHME)

1927-29
WINDMILL HILL , WILTSHIRE
Classification -Neolithic Causewayed enclosure
Auspice:Private
Funding:Private
Director:Alexander Keiller
Finds Holders: AKM & Devizes Museum

Archive: AKM

1933
THICKTHORN DOWN, EAST DORSET
Classification: Neolithic Long Barrow
Directors: Alexander Keiller/Charles Drew/Stuart Piggott
Finds Holders: Dorset County Museum, Dorchester
Archive: Dorset County Museum, Dorchester

1934
WEST KENNET AVENUE, WILTSHIRE
Classification: Neolithic Settlement
Auspice: Local Society (Wilts)
Directors: Alexander Keiller / Stuart Piggott
Finds Holders: Devizes Museum
Archive: AKM

1934-35
WEST KENNET AVENUE, WILTSHIRE
Classification: Standing Stone/burial
Auspice: Local Society (Wilts)
Funding: Private
Directors: Alexander Keiller / Stuart Piggott
Finds Holders: AKM
Archive: AKM/ Devizes

1934-35
WEST KENNET AVENUE, WILTSHIRE
Classification: Medieval Field System
Auspice: Local Society (Wilts)
Funding: Private
Directors: Alexander Keiller / Stuart Piggott
Finds Holders: AKM
Archive: AKM/ Devizes

1935
WINDMILL HILL , WILTSHIRE
Classification -Bronze Age Round Barrow
Auspice:Ministry of Works/National Trust
Funding: Ministry of Works/Private
Directors:Alexander Keiller / WEV Young
Finds Holders: AKM
Archive: AKM

1936
BADSHOT LEA, FARNHAM, SURREY
Classification - Neolithic Long Barrow
Auspice: Surrey Archaeological Society
Funding: Surrey Archaeological Society
Directors: Alexander Keiller / Stuart Piggott
Finds Holders: Guildford Museum /
Farnham Museum
Archive: Guildford Museum / Farnham
Museum

1936
LANHILL, CHIPPENHAM, WILTSHIRE
Classification: Neolithic Long Barrow
Auspice: Local Society (Wilts)
Funding: Private

Directors: Alexander Keiller / A D Passmore
Finds Holders: Devizes Museum/ Odontological Museum/Huntarian Museum, College of Surgeons, London
Archive: Devizes Museum Library, AKM,
Odontological Museum/Huntarian Museum, College of Surgeons, London

1937-39
WINDMILL HILL , WILTSHIRE
Classification -Period Uncertain, Round
Barrow/ burial
Auspice: National Trust/Ministry of Works
Funding: Ministry of Works/Private
Director :Alexander Keiller
Finds Holder: AKM
Archive: AKM / Devizes Museum/ NMRC,
Swindon (RCHME)

1937-39
AVEBURY STONE CIRCLE, WILT-
SHIRE
Classification: Neolithic Henge & Stone
Circle
Auspice: Private
Funding: Private
Director: Alexander Keiller
Finds Holder: AKM
Archive: AKM/ Devizes Museum Library/
NMRC, Swindon (RCHME)/ Salisbury &
South Wiltshire Museum

1939
WEST KENNET AVENUE, WILTSHIRE
Classification: Neolithic Standing Stone
Auspice: Local Society (Wilts)
Funding: Private
Directors: Alexander Keiller/ Stuart Piggott
Finds Holders: AKM
Archive: AKM, Salisbury & South Wiltshire
Museum

SURVEYS AND EXCAVATIONS IN NORTH EAST SCOTLAND

There is only one record of excavation by Keiller in Scotland, this being the report housed at the RCHMS in Edinburgh, entitled 'The Excavation of Cairn Ring Flats No.3'.

He completed over two hundred surveys of archaeological sites during the 1920s; a proportion of these surveys were included in the privately published 'Interim Report' and 'Final Report' as listed below. There is also at the RCHMS Manuscript 242, previously held by the Society of Antiquaries, Scotland, entitled Surveys of the Morven Cairn area, Aberdeenshire (Morven Burn, Peters Hill, Balmenach, Burn of Vat) 1924-5.

Interim Report upon such of the Stone Circles of Aberdeenshire and Kincardineshire as have been scheduled as Ancient Monuments

Auld Kirk, Graystone, Alford; Strone Hill (North Strone, Alford); Corr Stone Wood; Balgorkar or Castle Fraser; Loanhead, Daviot; Newcraig, Daviot; Tyrebagger; Cullerie/Leuchar/Standing Stones of Echt; Candle Hill, Insch; Dunnideer; Stonehead, Insch; Druidstone, Premnay; Inschfied; Aquhorthies; Cothiemuir, Castle Forbes/ Keig; Old Keig; Ardlair; Tuach Hill, Kintore; Midmar; Sunhoney; Tillyfourie/Whitehall Stone Circle, Bogmore Wood, Monymusk; Auchmacher, Old Deer; Candle Hill, Old Rayne; Candle Hill, Oyne/Hatton of Ardoyne; Loanend, Hawkhill; Milltown of Noth, Rhynie, Upper Ord Stone Circle and Upper Ord Standing Stone; Wheedlemont, Rhynie; Tomnagorn; Druidfield, Montgarrie; Tomnaverie.

Final Report upon such of the Stone Circles of Aberdeenshire and Kincardineshire as have been scheduled as Ancient Monuments

Corrydown, Auchterless; Logie Newton Circles, Auchterless; Mains of Hatton, Auchterless; Upperthird, Auchterless; Kirktown of Bourtie; Sheldon, Bourtie; Arn Hill, Cairnie; Netherton of Crimond/ Standing Stones of Netherton; Stonyfield, Drumblade; Cairnton, Forgue; Raich, Forgue; Yonder Bognie, Forgue; Hill of Fiddes, Foveran; Peathill, Keithall/ Peathill Standing Stone; Berrybrae, Lonmay; Monykebbuck, New Machar; Aiky Brae, Old Deer; Gaval, Old Deer/ Gaval Standing Stone; Loudon Wood, Old Deer/ Loudon Wood Stone Circle; White Cow Hill, Old Deer/ White Cow Wood; South Ythsie, Tarves.

LIST OF THE PUBLISHED WORKS OF ALEXANDER KEILLER

The Personnel of the Aberdeenshire Witchcraft Covens in the Years 1596-7. Privately reprinted 1922 by permission of the Editor of *Folklore* [This paper was not, however, originally published in *Folklore*]

'Witchcraft in Scotland.' *Folklore*, vol. 33 (1922), 303.

Library, Charles Street, London. 1923 [source- WA&NHS, Devizes, Wilts]

Interim Report upon such of the Megalithic Monuments of Aberdeenshire and Kincardineshire as have been Scheduled as Ancient Monuments. Compiled from the Morven Records. London (Vacher & Sons Ltd.), 1928.

Ibid. reprinted 1928.

Final Report upon such of the Megalithic Monuments..., 1928. [as per 'Interim Reports']

Wessex from the Air (with O. G. S. Crawford). Oxford, 1928.

'Excavation at Windmill Hill.' *Proceedings of the First International Congress of Prehistoric and Protohistoric Sciences, London, 1932.* Oxford, 1934, 135-8.

Megalithic Monuments of North-East Scotland. Paper read at a meeting of Section H of the British Association, 7 September 1934; reprinted for the Morven Institute of Archaeological Research, 1934.

'The Rock Shelter at Cap Blanc' (with D. Emerson Chapman). *Antiquity*, vol. 10 (1936), 207-9.

'Two Axes of Presely Stone from Ireland.' Ibid., 220.

'Recent Excavations at Avebury' (with Stuart Piggott). Ibid., 417-27.

'The Petrology of Stone Implements: Scheme for the Examination of Stone Specimens.' *Museums Journal*, vol. 37 (1937), 295-7.

'Excavation of an Untouched Chamber in the Lanhill Long Barrow' (with Stuart Piggott). *Proceedings of the Prehistoric Society*, vol. 4 (1938), 122-50.

'The January *Modern Mystic*: a Review.' *The Modern Mystic and Monthly Science Review*, vol. 3 (1939), 10ff.

'The Badshot Long Barrow' (with Stuart Piggott). *A Survey of the Prehistory of the Farnham District.* Surrey Archaeological Society, 1939, 133-49.

Guide to the Museum at Avebury, Wiltshire. Morven Institute of Archaeological Research, 1939.

'Avebury: Summary of Excavations, 1937 and 1938.' *Antiquity*, vol. 13 (1939), 223-33.

'The Chambered Tomb in Beowulf' (with Stuart Piggott). Ibid., 360-1.

'First Report of the Sub-Committee of the South-Western Group of Museums and Art Galleries on the Petrological Identification of Stone Axes' (with Stuart Piggott and F. S. Wallis). *Proceedings of the Prehistoric Society*, vol. 7 (1941), 50-72.

Catalogues – Ushabti and Egyptian Antiquities [source- Scottish National Gallery of Modern Art, Edinburgh]

BIBLIOGRAPHY

Berwick, GRG. 1957. A History of the Sizaire Berwick. *Motor Sport Magazine*, July Edition. 1957.

British Ski Yearbook. Published on behalf of the Ski Club of Great Britain. 1930, 1932, 1956

Burl, A. *Prehistoric Avebury.* Yale University. 1979

Burnett, D. *The Priestess of Henge.* London. 1982

Chitty, S.(Ed). *Antonia White Diaries 1926-1957.* Constable. 1991

Conway, H.G. *Grand Prix Bugatti* (2nd Ed.) Foulis. London,1983

Crawford, OGS. *Said and Done.* Weidenfeld and Nicolson. London , 1955

Cunnington, R.H. *From Antiquary to Archaeologist.* Shire Publications. Aylesbury, 1975

Daniels, G. & Chippindale, C. (Ed.). *The Pastmasters.* Thames & Hudson.

Davis, P. *Wheels Galore.* Rigby. Australia, 1981

Fletcher,D. *War Cars: British Armoured Cars in the First World War.* HMSO. London, 1987

Gould,R.T. *The Loch Ness Monster and Others.* Geoffrey Bles. London , 1934

Hawkes, CFC, Kendrick, TD. *Archaeology in England and Wales 1914-1931.* Methuen & Co. Ltd. 1932

Holroyd,M. *Augustus John Volume 2:The Years of Experience.* Heinemann. London, 1975

Hopkinson, Lyndall P, *Nothing to Forgive.* Chatto & Windus Ltd. London. 1988

Hutton, R. *The Pagan Religions of the Ancient British Isles.* BCA. 1991

Malone, C. *Avebury.* Batsford Press. 1989.

Mathew, W. M. *The Secret History of Guernsey Marmalade: James Keiller & Son Offshore.* La Societe Guernesiaise. Guernsey, 1998

Mathew, W.M. *Keiller's of Dundee: The Early Dynasty 1800-1879.* Abertay Historical Society, University of Dundee. Dundee, Forthcoming.

Mathew, W.M. *Keiller's of Dundee: The Collapse of the Dynasty 1879-1955.* Abertay Historical Society, University of Dundee . Dundee. Forthcoming.

Mawer,R. Sizaire-Berwick. *The Automobile Magazine.* July 1995/April 1996.

Mortimer, C. *With Hindsight.* Richard Methewood Ltd. 1991

Murray, M., *The Witch Cult in Eastern Europe.* OUP. Oxford, 1921

Olivier, E. *Edith Olivier: from her Journals 1924-1948.* Weidenfeld & Nicholson. London, 1990

Piggott,S. *Antiquity* 57. 1983

Piggott,S. *William Stukeley, An Eighteenth Century Antiquary.* Thames & Hudson. 1985.

Pitts, M. *Footprints through Avebury.* Digging Deeper. 1985

Sedgwick,M. (for Lord Montagu of Beaulieu) *Lost Causes of Motoring.* Cassell. London, 1969.

Ski Notes & Queries 1926. Published on behalf of the SCGB.

Smith, I. *Windmill Hill and Avebury.* OUP. London,1965

Stone, JFS. *Wessex.* Thames & Hudson. 1958.

Ucko P, Hunter M, Clarke A, David A. *Avebury Reconsidered.* Unwin Hyman Ltd. 1991

Wood, J. 1924 Hispano Suiza. *Classic Car Magazine,* August Edition. 1974.

INDEX